Fara Lynn Krasnopolsky was born in the rural village of Pochep, Russia, in the early 1900s. She earned a degree in law at the University of Kharkov, later emigrating to the United States with her husband. Since she couldn't use her degree in the States, her keen interest in music and drama led her to choose ballet as a career and she eventually became a professional dancer for The Metropolitan, as well as giving solo concerts in New York, Chicago, Canada and Moscow. She also established her own dance school where for twenty-five years she taught dance both as an art form and as exercise. Now in her eighties, she lives and writes in New York.

FARA LYNN KRASNOPOLSKY

I Remember

The Women's Press

First published in Great Britain by The Women's Press Limited 1992
A member of the Namara Group
34 Great Sutton Street
London EC1V 0DX

© Fara Lynn Krasnopolsky 1992

The right of Fara Lynn Krasnopolsky to be identified
as the author of this work has been asserted
by her in accordance with the Copyright, Designs
and Patents Act, 1988.

British Library Cataloguing in Publication Data:
A catalogue record for this book is available from the British Library.

ISBN 0 7043–4292 8

Phototypeset by Intype, London

Printed and bound in Great Britain by
Cox & Wyman Ltd, Reading

I dedicate this book to my husband, who was known as Michael but whom I called Monia. Though he did not know how to boil an egg, he was most supportive of all my early feminist undertakings. My gratitude goes out to his memory.

Acknowledgments

My special thanks to Suzanne McConell, who teaches fiction at Hunter College in New York City. She took a great interest in my manuscript, *I Remember*, and we spent many hours together discussing it.

My many thanks to Amanda Sebestyn, whose curiosity about my manuscript and love for it made its publishing in London possible.

Contents

Biographical Notes

'Neither in environment nor in heredity can I find the exact instrument that fashioned me.'
'Speak, Memory', Vladimir Nabokov

I was born in the first decade of the twentieth century, in a small Russian town called Pochep. My growing years were spent in a lower-middle-class Jewish family. Actually, we were poor, though my mother would not have liked to hear me say it. Our family consisted of Mother, always unhappy, Father, seldom at home, and a sister, four years older than I. It was she who managed to let me know how undesirable she found my arrival into this world.

Because of the Jewish quota in schools, I didn't enter the gymnazia at the usual age of six. Fortunately, always eager to learn, I was able to make up the two years I missed. As the younger child in a family preoccupied with problems of personal survival, my childhood was dismal, lonely and sad. I spent a lot of time alone, sitting on the stoop of our house waiting for someone to come home.

To entertain myself I developed a great sense of observation at an early age and began to imitate the speech and behaviour of the neighbours in our courtyard. This ability led me to pursue an acting career later.

While Russia was going through the First World War,

the Revolution, and finally, the process of being split
between the Bolsheviks, Mensheviks, and the White
Royal Guard, starvation was prevalent throughout the
land. The man who was destined to become my husband
paid his aunt a visit simply to eat. When Aunt Brocha,
who was also *my* aunt, invited my family to meet this
important relative from a big city – Petrograd – my
excitement was at its height.

I was thirteen and he ten years older. A graduate of
the Petrograd (now Leningrad) Conservatory, he had
been appointed to teach students to play the double-
bass in place of an absent professor, and finally was
named Professor himself. I was impressed beyond
words, and fell in love with him, his name – Monia –
his music, and the city he came from.

The meeting was brief. He left the following week,
having gained a few pounds, thanks to the hospitality
of our aunt. I continued dreaming, sighing and yearning.

The Revolution in Russia made my education uneven.
After various changes of government, the Bolsheviks
won, and Russia became the Soviet Union. My family
found itself in Kharkov, a university town in southern
Russia. I was still attending the gymnazia, with several
years to go before I was eligible for college.

Living in a big town was one of my dreams come
true. In spite of starvation and many other discomforts
that made life difficult in those years, I pursued roads
to a more fulfilling life: I studied Latin and French in
school, and dramatic art away from school.

During that first year in Kharkov my greatest sorrow
was not having a piano to play, and no money to buy
one. Then a neighbour, tired of looking at what he
considered an old broken-down upright, donated it to
the happiest girl alive. That waiting period remains the
only one in my memory when I lived without a piano.

At seventeen I graduated the eight levels from the
gymnazia, and since I couldn't enroll in college, because

there were no vacancies, I had a free year to look forward to. It was summer, and I decided this was the time to try to get into one of the better drama schools. With the little money I had saved from working part-time I went to Moscow. I had no extra money and no place to stay. I remember spending nights in the vestibules of expensive apartment buildings. Little did I realise that in the summer all the better schools were closed! I returned home to find my mother ill with typhus. Disheartened and guilt ridden, I believed I had been punished for thinking only of myself.

At that time one of my friends informed me that if I enrolled in an accelerated course to earn a law degree, I could become a Soviet lawyer. The offer was enhanced by a promise of a weekly *payok*, or ration, consisting of a loaf of bread and a herring for the duration of the course. Thus the family would immediately benefit from my educational adventure.

I spent a year cramming the history of Roman Law into my head at home and then spilling it out to the appointed professors by going to their homes for the exams. I never saw the university quarters, which for years remained unheated and in complete disorder. I then settled down to write the thesis necessary for my law degree.

I chose 'The history of Russian jurisprudence beginning with Peter the Great' as the subject of my thesis, and after two years of intensive research and swollen, frozen fingers (the library was also unheated), my labour was approved by the professor who supervised my work in progress. I must mention that all the education we were getting, as brief and painful as most of it was, had one big plus: it was *free* and, in a way, we got paid while learning.

My energy in those memorable days was inexhaustible. Despite starvation and the lack of any element of comfortable living, my desire to learn, to be, to become,

was limitless. While half of Russia was fighting for a
better life for all, the other half was dreaming and getting
ready for that dream to come true, by learning, discover-
ing, feeling and doing.

I went back to studying the piano with a teacher
whose knowledge of the instrument was as extensive
and as large as the woman herself was physically. I got
up daily at six o'clock, and burning a small light I
practised my lesson for two hours before going to work
as a part-time typist. My work allowed me to have a
meal a day at a public dining-room. The meal was free,
but I had to hold my nose to avoid smelling the stinking
soup that kept me alive. It also meant my mother had
one less mouth to feed. Several days a week after work
I studied poetry and plays at a drama school, still hoping
to become an actress some day.

All the while, people were dying daily, depending on
who was in power that day or week. If the White Guards
were gaining, then the Jews were the sacrificial lambs;
if the Red Army was winning then the conservatives, or
the reactionary royalists, were killed. My poor mother
never knew whether I was alive until I came home, late
at night. Life was exciting, but also often dangerous,
sad, and full of drama.

In the middle of all this the government, which had
become our landlord, told the family it would rent out
one of our rooms; our apartment was too large for one
family! So we quickly rented a room to two young girls.

One afternoon the girls announced that they were
expecting a guest: a young man from their home town,
Starodoub. At four o'clock the doorbell rang. I
answered the ring and opened the door to Monia, the
man I had met at Aunt Brocha's four years earlier, and
who still had a place in my heart. I ran to my room
yelling 'Where are my silk stockings?' I must have had
great faith in my legs in those days! But the gentleman
caller didn't even wait for my return. He disappeared

into the rented room. He emerged several hours later to be introduced to the family. Imagine that! He didn't remember having met us before. He eventually became a boarder, sleeping on a cot in the dining-room.

Monia, officially known as Mikhail Lvovich, was teaching at the Kharkov Conservatory and playing at the Opera House. My musical education began with free tickets to the opera. For a long time I thought that all operas were written and performed only in Russian.

Some months passed before I admitted to myself that I was in love. I became very jealous. I couldn't stand seeing him with another woman. I began to use lawyer's techniques to try to convince him of how blissful it would be to marry me. The effect I produced was exactly the opposite: he went home to his family in Starodoub. My sister, seeing me suffering from unrequited love, sent Monia a telegram saying that I was dying, and he suddenly reappeared.

His absence and his sudden return were noticed by all my friends, and I resumed my strong defence for marriage. My persuasion finally worked, and for two roubles I officially became Mrs Krasnopolsky. To please my parents and to make the marriage completely legal in their eyes, we had a Jewish ceremony, and a modest supper to celebrate the occasion. I remember that evening so well. My thesis adviser, a professor at the university, was present, and my husband got drunk on one glass of wine. He slept for most of the evening, much to the embarrassment of his eighteen-year-old wife.

As a wedding gift from my parents we were installed in a small room not far from them. The hall leading to the room was infested with roaches and mice but, for me, evenings filled with music from opera and concerts made everything else less important.

Shortly after our marriage Monia gave a successful concert at the Kharkov public library, with the noted Nikolay Malko conducting. Solo concerts on the bass

were rare. The only known soloist at that time was
Sergey Koussevitsky. My husband began dreaming of
doing concerts in Europe. His two brothers had been
living in America for a number of years and an invitation
from them was the only way to get out of the Soviet
Union. His desire was understandable; his monthly
salary for teaching at the conservatory paid only for a
coffee and pastry for the two of us in a coffee shop. I
was offered a job as a Soviet lawyer at the same time as
he received the invitation from his brothers to come to
America.

The exodus from the Soviet Union had assumed epi-
demic proportions: rich people were leaving out of fear;
artists and musicians in the hope of getting wider recognition of their talents. But most of the latter group were
leaving for Paris; America was for the uneducated and
culturally limited, not for the 'intelligentsia', or at least
so it appeared to people of my generation. Monia
believed that going to America was the only way he
could get to Europe. I had to decide whether to join
him or remain in Russia. My decision had serious impli-
cations: Monia was all set for a brilliant career in music,
even if it meant losing me, a possibility that didn't seem
to frighten him. I had either to follow him or lose a
husband. Follow him I did.

Seeing Europe for the first time, I had many exciting
moments. I remember my ecstasy at seeing the ocean in
the port city of Riga. I remember shedding tears when
I first heard music in a restaurant and saw people eating
while the musicians were playing – I was so offended
for them.

When we landed in Chicago after spending several
months in Europe, waiting for a visa, I suddenly
realised, in a most traumatic way, how far I was from
everything I knew and loved. Separated from my family
for the first time, I had to live in a strange country
whose language I did not speak. Having no money of

our own, we had to live with Monia's mother, two sisters and a younger brother. The only connection I had with them was their disapproval of our marriage.

In the 'good old days', immigrants, who came to America in droves, began their climb to riches by working in factories. I was too frail to try factory work, weighing only 105 pounds. I began to suffer from the early symptoms of a nervous breakdown. To practise law I would have had to spend years learning the language, and then take the bar exam, both of which seemed insurmountable to a young, undernourished, under-everything young girl from Pochep.

Fortunately, the language of music being universal, Monia found a job in a movie theatre, playing for live show after the movie. We moved to a room in a privately owned apartment and decided to seek a doctor's advice about my health. Having a child was my only road to mental and physical health, so they said. So we tried. A son was born. We named him Yuri. But the symptoms of shattered nerves did not disappear. I came to a secret conclusion: finding something to do outside the family was the best cure. Pursuing my interest in acting was my first choice, but language was a barrier again. A friend came to my aid. She knew of a dance class conducted by a famous Russian dancer; and so I became the most ardent pupil of the Adolph Bolm School of Dance, practising at home when not at the class, using my son's crib as the *barre*. After two years of intensive study, I felt I had all the prerequisites to become a professional dancer.

By that time my husband had become a member of the Chicago Symphony. The orchestra played for the Metropolitan Opera's summer season in Ravinia Park, a suburb of Chicago. Ruth Page was the choreographer for the Met and I spent six good summers dancing with its ballet corps. It was healthy for the children to be in the country, and thanks to our social graces half the

Chicago population also had a chance to spend good weekends there. I should mention that by then I had managed, with a little help from my husband, to give birth to a beautiful little girl whom we named Mara. That incident, in the middle of my preparation for a dance career, made me particularly careful thereafter not to over-populate the USA.

Now for the highlights of my professional life: after my stage experience under the Metropolitan's auspices, I gave my first concert at the Diana Court in Chicago, consisting of dances I had choreographed myself. It was reviewed by Glen Dillard Gunn, then the music critic of the *Chicago Herald Examiner*. I quote portions of it with pride:

> This young woman is one of the most interesting dancers. She has all the technique of her art as it has been developed by the moderns in that department: somewhat vaguely known as 'interpretative.' Better still, she has so much imagination and so great is her power of suggestion that I confidently expect her to enlarge its vocabulary, now limited, too often, by the personalities that practice it. Her translation of the familiar Negro spiritual 'Nobody Knows the Trouble I've Seen' into terpsichorean terms, was deeply expressive. It had grace, eloquence, variety and beauty of feeling which is, at least, the finest kind of beauty.

The following year I gave a successful concert in Moscow, at the Lunacharsky Theatre, after which the *Gosisdat* (the government Bureau of Arts Management) offered me a concert tour, which, unfortunately, did not materialise because of Stalin's paranoid fear of foreigners. When I heard from the Gosisdat that they would not send me a contract for the tour they had offered me, I was heartbroken. My dance career seemed at a dead end. The year was 1935.

Chicago went through a typically rough spring and

the rare sunshine was welcomed by all. I heard from fellow dancers that Bennington College, in Bennington, Vermont was having a special summer course in modern dance for professional dancers trained in ballet technique. This looked like something that could revive my hope in myself and in the world.

I made all kinds of arrangements to have the children in summer camps, borrowed money to pay for the summer at Bennington College, and it proved to be everything I had hoped for: the teaching staff consisted of the greatest talents in modern dance – Graham, Humphrey, Weidman, Hania Holm, José Limon and Lewis Hurst.

I worked hard and was selected to do a solo at a concert given at Bennington by Anna Sokolov. I realised that the vocabulary of modern dance was much more expressive than classical ballet. I called my dance 'Hunger' and composed it using the newly acquired dance language. I was pleased with its success.

The atmosphere among the students and teachers was full of friendly assistance, and frequent discussions were of great help. I was glad to have found a good friend in Lewis Hurst, and I remember how he influenced me when he said: 'If you want to dance, you have to come to New York'.

When I returned home, Chicago looked and felt worse than ever. I had never liked the town, and at the time I lived there I thought of it as a big city with small-town manners. To find places in which to dance was most difficult and my association with the greatest in the modern dance field that summer had made everything I undertook seem puny and uninteresting; besides, it didn't pay much. I dreamed of the summer that had passed so fast.

None the less, I continued my association with Ruth Page, dancing with her company at the Goodman Theater in Chicago and touring throughout Canada and in

New York. I dreamed of living in New York. This frequently expressed desire irritated my husband, and since he had a good job playing on a big radio station he would not consider dropping everything and running to New York. 'For what?' he said. It always ended in an argument. Life seemed unbearable. One day I picked up my children and left for New York, where nothing but a dream was waiting for me.

No money, no place to stay, no job. I couldn't even take a dance class with my idol, Martha Graham at that time. I knew a kindly aunt of Monia's who lived all the way uptown. It was a clean and friendly place, and I would be able to leave the children there while I took a dance class. When I told the family of my predicament, they kindly invited us to stay with them.

I renewed my contact with some of the dancers I had met in Bennington, found out that a Work Projects Association (WPA) dance project was being formed by the government, auditioned for it, and was accepted. I had to conceal the fact that I had children; it seemed a small price to pay.

I asked my husband to send me some money for the children's support, and the three of us moved happily to West 52nd Street, the noisiest of night-club neighbourhoods, where night turned into day, and fighting and murders were *de rigueur*. But in the daytime the best private school provided the children with a good education.

It makes me dizzy now to think of the schedule I devised for myself: morning rehearsals on the project (except weekends), a daily class in modern dance technique with Graham, a composition class weekly with Lewis Hurst and, in between, cooking and shopping.

Fortunately, we shared the apartment with a young girl dancer who agreed to baby-sit for me whenever I wanted to see a dance recital. I also worked several evenings a week at Anna Sokolov's studio, composing my own dances.

Monia did send some money, but his letters were full of remorse and loneliness. I began to feel guilty – depriving my children of his presence – and, secretly, a fear of never again knowing love and attention made me feel frozen inside, until my belief in myself as a woman amounted to zero.

Six months later Monia appeared unannounced on the threshold at 52nd Street, just as he had done when I was seventeen in Kharkov. Frankly, I was glad that somebody wanted me enough to leave a lucrative position on the radio, to have to start a new career, a new life. The time for this was not propitious. America was suffering the most severe depression. There were long lines of people waiting to get a plate of soup or a loaf of bread. Unemployment was at its height. But President Franklin Roosevelt did the right thing – workers' projects flourished, everyone eager to contribute; hope shone in everyone's eyes, and the country discovered a lot of talent.

We moved again. This time our friends were people who, when drunk, seemed to be able to get to their homes on Charles Street only through our apartment. Nevertheless, as a family we flourished. Monia found a job at a small Jewish radio station. I was still on the WPA project, so our marriage and the visible results of it, our two children, had to be kept a secret. This illicit twist we were young enough to enjoy.

Helen Tamiris, a well-known dancer, headed the WPA Dance Project. She choreographed a ballet named *How Long, Brethren*, based on Negro spirituals. It ran successfully on Broadway for two months, boosted by good reviews. The children were also tasting the sweet fruit of success. Yuri got a scholarship at the Henry Street Music School. Mara had a scholarship at Madame Walter's, a prestigious drama school at Carnegie Hall.

Monia graduated to a higher position, playing in the Radio City Music Hall Orchestra. It also meant more money. We moved to a bigger apartment. Mara was getting old enough to merit her own room, but Mamma and Papa still had to sleep in the living-room.

Alas, nothing lasts forever. Dancers were among the first to lose their jobs. Moneywise it was not a great loss, but psychologically the void was tremendous. Meanwhile, Germany's march on the world continued and Russia was threatened. Next, my sister died, due to lack of penicillin in Russia. Mother was left alone, and we wanted to bring her to America.

This was not a simple procedure. A lot of paperwork and, of course, money were involved as well as another move to a bigger apartment with a room for Mother. Sunnyside was our choice. It was as close to a suburb as we could afford and as near as we wanted to be to New York. This change took two years to accomplish and then we were able to enjoy it for only two years. Mother came. Poor Mara lost her independence as she had to share a bedroom with her after all. Still, we felt richer and happier, though not for long. Some insane tenant couldn't stand Yuri's practising, and renewal of our lease was refused. We looked for another apartment but each time, as soon as we mentioned piano practising, we were turned down.

We bought a house. I had never wanted to be an owner of a house, nor did we have the money to buy one. We had to beg and borrow. For six months after we moved – until we had paid back all the friends who had lent us money for the house – I couldn't even have a new pair of stockings. Jackson Heights was our new address. The area had been a golf course, but developers had got the land and built terraced houses. There was a little garden at the back, and what made the house attractive to us above all was an apple tree growing in the garden. It was a three-storey house, with three bedrooms. For the first time in my life I had a bedroom. What luxury, even though I had to share it with my husband. Another big attraction was the basement. The minute I saw it I began to dream of my own studio – to work, compose and dance in. We bought three wall mirrors, installed *barres* and, with great difficulty, covered the floor with a heavy linoleum suitable for dancing.

Even though I was frequently called a feminist before the term was widely used, I found the struggle of combining performing with playing the roles of wife and mother difficult, and the weariness was beginning to show. I decided to settle down with a dance school of my own, now that I had a studio.

I devised a programme that would educate students to know dance as an art form as well as experiencing it as an exercise. For over twenty-five years I imbued children and adults with the love of dance as an art, building audiences as well as dancers, and frequently including music that had evolved in connection with dance forms.

When I found out that to teach dance in college one had to have a master's degree, I enrolled on an evening course in order to get one. The courses were all taught by European professors who had fled from Nazi Germany. I received an MA in Sociology after a year of study at the New School for Social Research, and spent two years writing another thesis, this one in English, entitled, 'American Dance Between the Two World Wars'. Strangely, having earned the master's degree, I discovered that teaching dance in a college was not what I wanted to do at all. So I continued teaching in two schools of my own, one in Jackson Heights, the other in Roslyn, Long Island, until a doctor discovered that I was suffering from a mild heart disease which made it painful for me to demonstrate certain steps during classes.

I had to stop teaching. Both schools were closed, and a little while later I chose Hunter College in New York City, first to expand my knowledge of French, and, the following year, to learn the craft of writing. I had always loved to write, but at Hunter I began to learn how.

The experiences described in the stories are biographical vignettes dug up from the bank of memories, fictionalised and woven, to give me a flexibility with facts and time. The need to go back to 'the way we were', that is, to write about a particular childhood, came from a realisation that each new road discovered and loved by me was uniquely evoked, not by role models, but by invisible cords from within.

Certain people and opportunities helped, of course, to bring the hidden cravings to the surface. I hope that this slim volume will inspire others, for I believe that each one of us has at least one story to tell.

I Remember

I remember the first me: I was three years old. We were rushing home. Papa carried me in his arms. We heard singing from afar. Papa was saying, 'They are still singing revolutionary songs.' I could smell my father's Derby hat. It smelled good. I liked being carried by Father. He never carried me again.

I remember sounds and smells. Mother told me much later: 'We were returning from a visit with Aunt Brocha. The songs: they were leftovers from the social upheavals of that year, 1905.'[1]

Next, I remember me at five, always following my sister, Raya, around. She was four years older and didn't want to be followed. She yelled, 'Mamma.'

Mother came to the door, looking big and angry. I stopped following my sister and slowly turned back. Mother stopped me, took my hand and explained; 'Raya is a big girl, you are still little. Stop running after her.'

I felt thin and scrawny. My eyes were full of tears. I asked Mamma, 'Why are you always busy?' She smiled, but didn't answer. 'And Papa, why is he never home?'

Mamma explained, 'He has to travel to sell furs.'

I remained sitting alone on the stoop of the house, waiting for someone to come back. The years from three to five were the loneliest years of my life. Everybody gave me reasons why I must stay behind, waiting for their return.

The me at six. I was full of hope. I asked Mother when we were going to the gymnazia to register me. Summer was almost over.

'We'll go next Monday, I promise,' Mother assured me.

On Monday we put our good clothes on and went to meet with Maria Valerianovna, the principal of the gymnazia. She was a short, very fat woman, who sat most of the time because it was hard for her to walk. She told us very politely, 'I regret to have to tell you that the Jewish quota for this year is complete. Come next year.'

Mamma looked upset. She said, 'Thank you,' to the principal, and turned to me saying, 'To be Jewish is to have problems. Raya had to start school in a lower grade because the date on her birth certificate was wrong. Thank goodness she was good enough in school to skip a year.'

We returned home disappointed. But Mamma didn't give up. Not on the subject of education. She liked to tell us, whenever she had the time, how important education was. 'I didn't have a chance to be educated, but the two of you will.' She continued talking even when we were not listening.

She had an idea: to get a teacher of Hebrew who could teach us the meaning of the prayers and the language in general.

So we now had a teacher who came twice a week. Her name was Chayca. I remember her well. She had black hair, a very pleasant smile, and she wore shiny black boots laced all the way up from her ankles. My sister seemed uninterested, but I tried to learn all I could.

The big Jewish holiday arrived – Yom Kippur (the Day of Atonement). It is the most important holiday for Jewish people. They cry and they fast on that day.

Too young to fast, I was allowed to eat. My sister could also eat but she pretended she was old enough to fast.

Mamma put on her good clothes, ate some rice, had a glass of tea and began her tearful goodbyes before leaving for the synagogue, as if we would never see her again. We all felt very sad. She kissed me and my sister and wished us a good year. Her nose was red and her eyes teary. I wondered. Was it possible that she had angered God and was afraid that He'd punish her? I went to bed crying.

The following morning Mother went to the synagogue very early. I was sorry to see her go alone, but Papa didn't get back from his travels for this holiday since it lasted only one day.

At noon my sister and I went to visit her. We saw her full of tears again. I decided to let God enter my life. Maybe when the two of us prayed and observed all the rules, He would show Mother, somehow, a way to His heart. I knew so little about God. Did He have a heart?

I prayed three times a day. I remembered to kiss the mezuzah[2] at bedtime. One night I jumped out of bed, a cold sweat covering my body. I felt as if a herd of animals had attacked me, screaming, 'You are forgetting, you are forgetting.' I ran to touch the sacred piece of parchment, the mezuzah, attached to the doorway. Not being tall enough, I reached it only by getting up on my tiptoes.

I learned the rules for believers. There were a lot of regulations to remember about food: no milk or its products to be had for six hours after one had meat of any kind. The Hebrew language was not an easy language to remember, and Chayca was a strict teacher. All of this made me think a lot.

The autumn holidays were over. The cold winter days were passing too. Soon I'd be seven. Still no gynmazia.

I could read a little Russian now, picking it up here and there.

Mother kept looking at me. 'Hannah, you are too thin. Are you well? Are you eating enough?' She sounded worried. We went to the doctor.

After the examination I heard the doctor say, 'She has an ulcer. It should be treated with a strict diet.'

Mother didn't understand. 'What kind of a diet, Doctor?'

'Plenty of milk and a lot of butter.' For some reason Mother began to cry. I was afraid to ask her why she was crying. Everything seemed to be wrong. I wanted to run away. Instead, I cleaned, washed and scrubbed, trying to help Mother.

Because of the very rich diet, Mamma and I argued a lot about the six-hour food law. She told me that maybe God had more important things to do than to watch for the legal entrance of milk into one's stomach. Mother's answer finished our argument about milk versus meat. She declared, 'According to God, it is important to listen to Mother.'

I loved the early morning light that came into one room only in our house. I opened my eyes. Maybe today will be the good day I prayed for. I heard Mamma singing. If the song was a sad one, it would make me want to close my eyes and not get up at all. But today, Mamma was singing a happy song. I jumped out of bed.

As I drank my morning tea, Mamma told me the good news.

'Today we will go to see the Russian tutor. She teaches at the gymnazia, but she also likes to help Jewish children to enter school. For a little money Elizaveta Petrovna can make you sound very smart.' As Mother told this to me, she made a sign meaning, 'It's a secret between you and me'.

I enjoyed learning to read and write. The tutor didn't teach me anything new, but Mamma told me that

Elizaveta Petrovna would make it possible to register me in the first class of the gymnazia.

I liked going to the lessons. First, I entered a small garden full of fragrant flowers, then rang the bell to the tutor's house. Elisaveta Petrovna usually met me at the door. Her face was covered in white powder. I loved the smell of it.

The *me* at eight, and even at eight and a half, I remember only too well. I felt almost as old as my sister, and was surprised when she reminded me that she was still four years older. It was my second year in school. Everything needed adjustment: religion and food. My ulcer was healing, but milk still waited six hours after eating meat. Religion and school. We had school six days a week, including the Sabbath. I knew that to carry books on that day was forbidden. I had the idea of forming a human chain of six Jewish girls standing two feet apart, each throwing the books to the next in line; then, the one who was first would run to the end of the chain, thus avoiding carrying the books. We had fun doing it, and I knew that God saw all and would give me a high mark for finding a game by which to observe His laws.

Dear Diary

I can only let your eyes see this. I am upset and disappointed. You will not believe it, but I'll tell you anyhow. After everything I did to please God, like kissing the mezuzah before going to sleep, no milk after meat before the six hours, in addition to praying three times a day, and learning geography, which I hate, I came home with a note saying that I must have a re-examination in geography before I can pass to the next class.

When I read the note from the principal to Mamma, she heaved a heavy sigh, wiped her nose and mouth

with the long cotton apron she wore when doing house-
work, and said: 'I hope it doesn't mean that you have
to repeat all of last year's schooling. Do you know how
much it would cost?' She sounded angry at me, at school
or maybe even at God.

I tried to defend myself. 'Mamma,' I said, 'I studied
geography even though I disliked it. All the places sound
so far away and we'll probably never see them. Will I
ever swim in any of the oceans? I am even afraid to go
near the river.'

Mother didn't look convinced. I had to try harder.

'Wouldn't you think that observing all of God's laws
and remembering the names of the five continents would
be enough?'

Suddenly a miracle! Worry lifted from Mamma's face.
'Hannah, I know what we should do. We'll ask Elisaveta
Petrovna to tutor you in geography. They always like
to earn a little extra money, and who doesn't? And from
whom, if not from Jews? Maybe that was the reason
she didn't pass you. Would we ever complain? Schooling
is so important. Without an education, what are you?'

Mother sounded relieved. I promised to get the
teacher's address again in school. On the first day of
the summer vacation both of us, wearing our good
clothes, were in front of a small garden leading to the
teacher's house. Mamma made me wait in the garden
while she talked about the cost. Elisaveta Petrovna
agreed to give me five lessons for fifteen roubles. Since
it would be she who would also question me at the re-
examination, the guarantee that I would pass the exam
was included.

On Monday, at eleven o'clock, I was again in front
of Elisaveta Petrovna's house, scared to face her. She
opened the door herself. The skin on her face was full
of little holes. She used a lot of powder to cover them,
and she smelled like my Aunt Brocha. I recognised the

smell – *Lebiaji Puch* powder. It made me less afraid of her.

During the five lessons she made me learn a lot about the town we lived in, and at the re-examination, when she asked me: 'Describe your town geographically', I recited all I had learned and will probably never forget.

'Pochep is the Administrative Centre of the Pochep Rayon, Briansk Oblast. It is situated on the Sudost River, a tributary of Desna. Pochep has a railway station on the Bryansk–Unecha Line, eighty-four kilometres south-west of Bryansk.'

'Do you know of a town close to Pochep that is well known geographically?' asked the teacher.

'Yes,' I answered. 'I know of one town, because my uncle lives there.'

I noticed that all three teachers present were smiling.

'Continue,' said my examiner.

'The name of that town is Pahar. It was called Rado-goshch until the seventeenth century. It was also an urban settlement, located on the Sudost River. Pahar was burned in the sixteenth century, four times, during the wars between Russia and Poland. This probably accounts for its name.[3]

Dear Diary,

After I passed the re-examination, I had a very serious discussion with God. Of course, I did all the talking, but very respectfully. After all, God knows what He is doing, even though we don't always know. I will never look at a geography book again. I am beginning to drink milk after eating meat. Mother is glad to see the change in my eating habits.

'You are too young to observe *all* God's laws,' she commented.

School is becoming a very important part of my life. I like almost all the subjects except for two – geography and embroidery. I am glad to know a little more about the town I live in but the rest of it is just cold names to me. As for embroidery, even watching the girls doing it makes me sleepy. My most favourite subjects are literature and maths, the first because by reading Pushkin, Lermontov and Krylov, I learn a lot about love and suffering, the second, because it makes me think.

My ulcer is gone, helped by the doctor, and by a rich diet of milk and butter. But I am still very thin and can't seem to grow the way other girls in school do. I hope some day soon to skip a year or two. I might feel more grown-up then. My sister still considers me a baby. She wants her friends to call her Raisa. She thinks it sounds more important than the short version, *Raya.*

A Visit to an Aunt

It was one of the hottest summers in Pochep. In the evening people would sprawl on the footsteps of their houses, just to cool off. One day, on 15 July to be exact, when the heat seemed at its peak, Mamma called me and my sister Raya, and said, 'How would you like to visit your Aunt Chaya-Esther and cool off at the same time?'

I, so glad to hear that something would be done about the heat, ran to Mother, hugged her, and yelled, 'Go to Panurovca? Oh, yes. When can we go? We've never been there. When can we go, Mamma?'

The day before, on the fourteenth, I had just turned ten. Neither I nor anyone else celebrated my birthday, but I felt almost as grown up as my sister, though she was four years older. No 'yes' from her about the trip as yet. Meanwhile, Mother and I were busy discussing what we should take along, hoping that eventually Raya would say 'Yes', and would come too.

Since none of us owned huge wardrobes, the question of luggage didn't take too much time. Mamma suggested: 'We'll travel in our everyday dresses and take the "good" dresses along. Frankly,' she added, 'I don't know where one would wear a "good" dress in Panurovca.'

I didn't agree with Mother (silently, of course). In minutes, I imagined places for picnics with friends, visits with farmers who ate their meals outdoors in their own beautiful gardens, and everywhere we would wear our good dresses. I liked to make up things, to invent them. Mamma would say, 'Hannah, you are a dreamer'.

Raya was elected to write a letter to Aunt Chaya-Esther, telling her that we wished to see her. It wouldn't be nice, Mamma said, if we told her that the heat was driving us away from home. Mamma called it being 'diplomatic'. Besides, she really wanted to see her sister, but was looking for more than one reason for visiting, since travel was expensive.

A reply came sooner than expected. It was a short note, though it did include a real invitation. Aunt Chaya-Esther wrote that she heard how hot it was in Pochep and assured Mother of a pleasant stay in Panurovca.

Papa had not been approached as yet. If he agreed to let us go, it would be up to Mamma, anyway, to scrape up enough money for the undertaking.

We went by train to Bryansk where we were met by Uncle Hirch, Aunt's husband. He was a tall man and looked like a gypsy with his swarthy complexion and black beard, and dressed in a white shirt with a belt. He came in a roomy wagon, in which he usually brought his vegetables to the city market to be sold. It was pulled by a tired old horse. My sister, Raya, made a face when she saw the modest vehicle. I was delighted to ride in a peasant wagon without a top so that the whole world could see us and we, in turn, had a chance to see the surroundings of Panurovca. The road from the station to the cottage was lined with birch and oak trees. Occasionally we could see a farmer's home. The road was dusty, which prevented me from seeing much.

Aunt Chaya-Esther was one of Mother's older sisters. The last time we had seen her was when she had come for a visit to Pochep six years before. I was very little then. She still had black hair and nice skin, but her teeth grew crooked for some reason and that spoiled her smile. She met us at their small cottage, in front of which three birch trees stood proudly. Their smooth white bark made the whole place look cheerful and protected.

After the customary greetings, Raya ran over to Mother and whispered: 'We aren't going to stay here, Mamma, are we?'

With a look of surprise, Mamma answered, 'Of course we are.' When all of us went inside, Aunt Chaya-Esther looked a little apologetic. Maybe she felt that we were comparing Panurovca with Pochep. Raya and Mamma were on the warpath. I seemed to be the only one who wanted to examine everything.

I walked through the house. There were only two rooms in it. One served as a kitchen, dining and resting room. The other was a bedroom for Aunt and Uncle. The two rooms were separated by a door. Between the kitchen and the entrance to the house was an open oven where all the meals were cooked. The bedroom had one wooden bed, which was covered with a light yellow blanket. In the other room stood a long table, heavy enough to be of oak. It was covered with an oilcloth full of painted birds. I liked the birds. They made the table look inviting and hospitable.

When we brought in our modest luggage, Aunt Chaya-Esther announced, 'This is the only place we have for you to sleep.' She was pointing to the floor. 'We'll cover it with heavy blankets. All three of you can sleep together.' Then, as if to soften the blow of the sleeping arrangements, she asked if we were hungry.

'I am, Aunt,' said Raya. She was offered black bread, some butter and a glass of milk. Aunt Chaya-Esther proudly announced that the milk and butter came from their own cow.

I went to look at the garden. I was very glad to have recognised most of the growing vegetables. The cucumbers, peas and corn were still in bloom. The delicate flowers looked full of promise.

When I returned to the house, I heard Raya asking Aunt Chaya-Esther if any of her friends had daughters of her age. 'Yes,' answered Aunt, 'I know one Jewish family who has a very nice girl about your age, and they live not very far from here.' She added: 'They own a farm. I'll take you there to meet her.'

Mamma spent the afternoon exchanging news with her sister about their relatives: one cousin had a new baby, another had just got married, and some distant relative had died. I listened to their conversation and realised how seldom the two sisters shared in either the festivities or the grief of their relatives.

I heard Mother say, 'Who has the money to travel from one place to another?' Mamma looked sad as she said it and I felt sorry for her.

Raya wanted to take a walk in the forest nearby. Surprisingly, she asked me to go with her, which made me feel an inch taller. When I heard her say, 'Come Hannah, we'll walk in the first forest we see,' I ran and tried to take hold of her hand, but she pulled it away and said, 'Don't hang on to me, Hannah, I walk faster than you.' Still, I was glad to be with her.

When we came across wild red berries growing in abundance Raya picked up some wide leaves from the trees, and throwing them to me said, 'Here, you carry the berries in these to the cottage.'

I suddenly felt hurt, as if all the past years of neglect from Raya had been thrown in my face and covered me with mud. I clenched my fists, picked up the fallen berries from the ground and promised myself to pay her back some day. That made me feel better. I gave Raya a crooked smile, but lovingly carried the picked berries and didn't try to keep pace with her any more.

On the way back, Raya kept on talking: 'I'll be glad to tell Mamma and Papa, especially Papa, that I took care of "Baby Hannah". I took her for a walk. I don't like anything here, nothing, nobody.'

After the first walk, I had to pick berries alone. My sister flatly refused to go with me. I was trying so hard to make my sister a friend, but the four years' difference between us built a wall that she refused to climb over. This made me madder and madder every time she walked away with her friends and left me alone.

Panurovca was a very small village. In the centre of it stood a big well, and on my walks I saw people carrying water from the well to their homes. Our aunt's cottage was very modest. Aunt Chaya-Esther seemed to be satisfied with the way things were. When she talked about her life she said, 'Now that Rivka [her daughter] is married and lives in Mglin, the cottage is enough for the two of us. Hirch sells enough vegetables so we are able to buy the other things we need.' And she ended with: 'I am so glad you came for a visit.'

As for me, I'd like to tell her, 'Yes, Aunt Chaya-Esther, we like it very much, except for the nights.' The nights were not very pleasant. The coverings on the floor were inadequate. The floor remained hard. I, being the smallest, had to fight the hardest for some space on the floor. When dawn came, I would hear the buzzing of the flies which was like music to me, as it heralded the arrival of morning.

On the third day, or perhaps it was on the fourth, the three of us and Aunt Chaya-Esther all put on our good dresses and went to call on the Rivkins, the neighbours who had a girl Raya's age. Their farm looked like a palace compared to our aunt's hut. The corners of the four steps we climbed to the guest entrance of the house were decorated with pots of geraniums. We opened the door to the hall and saw a mirror, on either side of which were stuffed elk's heads with horns used as coat hangers.

Mrs Rivkin, a nice, plumpish woman, met us at the

hall with a pleasant 'hello' and ushered us into a large sitting-room filled with a number of soft chairs and two sofas. Mrs Rivkin led us to one of them. I sat down along with the others and almost disappeared into the softness of the sofa's contents.

Their daughter, Lena Rivkin, was obviously very glad to meet Raya, and after just a nod to me and to all the Mammas, took Raya away, probably to her room. When Mrs Rivkin asked if we would like to see the rest of the house, I jumped up first. There were separate rooms for every need and every purpose; a large kitchen with a huge oven where one could roast a whole goose; on the walls of the kitchen hung many copper pots of different sizes. The dining-room had two buffets, one for storing china and linen, the other for serving food. All this Mrs Rivkin explained very slowly and competently, being obviously in the habit of conducting tours for guests. A large round table was placed in the middle of the room and the chairs all around it looked inviting.

The bedrooms followed, one for herself and her husband, and one for their daughter, where we saw Lena and Raya. They looked as though they were having fun. My heart must have missed a beat for I again felt neglected by my sister. Could it be only the age difference, or does she really hate me? I wondered. Mrs Rivkin led us to a guest-room. Oh, what luxury! Here we wouldn't have to sleep on the floor. We returned to the living-room, where this time I noticed the beautiful lace curtains, and two ficus trees hugging the large windows.

After the long-winded tour, Mrs Rivkin offered us a glass of tea. Wishing to appear polite, we refused it. 'It's too hot to drink it,' said Mamma, laughing at her own joke.

We did accept and also enjoyed a piece of cake. 'Home-made,' Mrs Rivkin assured us.

Raya and Lena Rivkin tried to separate themselves from the protective umbrella of the family. I stayed outdoors mostly. The Rivkins had a garden filled abundantly with sunflowers, roses and other flowers, the names of which I didn't even know.

Mamma called us, saying, 'Let's not wear out our welcome.'

They said their goodbyes and Raya made an appointment with Lena for the next day. I tried to remind my sister of my existence and asked, 'What about our picking berries, Raya?'

'You'll pick them yourself,' came her answer.

Picking berries with my sister was by far the most enjoyable outing for me. I became acquainted for the first time with squirrels, birds, worms and frogs, as well as with other creatures of the forest world.

The vegetable garden near Aunt's house became another happy diversion. I examined each growing plant and praised the ones that had shown some growth since I had last seen them. Yet it was lonely doing this alone. I missed having a friend of my own.

Every night before falling asleep I secretly kept on repeating: 'Nobody wants me, nobody wants me.'

Once, my mother heard my mumbling, but she did not ask me why I was crying. She said, 'Hannah, you are such a moody child. Go to sleep.'

The days were passing quickly despite the small discomforts. 'But it isn't as hot as it would have been at home,' Mamma reminded us; and 'I heard someone say that sleeping on the floor is good for one's back' – that came from Aunt Chaya-Esther.

For me, the buzzing flies were still a welcome sound and sight. In just a few more days we would have to start getting ready for the journey home.

One morning, after my sister had left to see her new friend, Lena, I put on my good dress and, unnoticed by anyone, left the house. At first I walked slowly, as if I had to complete a plan of action. Gradually, however, my pace increased and then I ran the rest of the way until I arrived at the Rivkin farm. When I opened the door to the house and asked for Raya, I was out of breath.

Raya came in from the garden where she had been talking to Lena. 'What's the matter, Hannah, why did you come?' she asked.

'Father came to see us and when I told him where you were he asked me to go and bring you back as soon as possible,' I said. By this time the rest of the Rivkins had gathered around, fearing that some bad news had brought me to them in such a hurry.

But Raya couldn't believe her ears. 'You mean Papa came here just to see us and asked especially for me?'

Raya's surprise was justified. Father had never shown any particular interest in her, and the demand for her immediate presence could be questioned.

My love for exaggerating a story to make it splendid-sounding took hold of me when I saw four pairs of eyes watching me eagerly and waiting to hear more about Papa's arrival in Panurovca.

I continued: 'He drove in about an hour ago in a fancy carriage pulled by two white horses. The *kutcher* wore a very rich uniform, full of gold braid. And you know how well Papa dresses, usually. His luggage was also beautiful and expensive looking. When he got off the train, his red beard waving in the breeze, he looked so much like the Tzar that people began running after the carriage, greeting him, begging him for favours. Some even complained about having so little land and no food. They called him all the endearing names they could think of – *batushka* (our father), *rodimi* (our own), *milenki* (darling), *spasitel nash* (our saviour), 'and he, of course, was beaming and waving, looking pleased, as if he was used to these demonstrations of affection.'

'Hannah, let's go,' cried Raya. 'Papa is waiting to see me and you are wasting time here.'

Raya's excitement was natural, but when I saw the

Rivkins listening with their mouths open in disbelief, I was in my glory. But I had to stop my monologue when my sister grabbed my arm and the two of us practically flew away from the farm after a quick goodbye.

We ran all the way home. When we opened the door to the cottage, it was empty. I slowed down to remain in the rear. My sister ran through every corner looking for her father, or for something that belonged to him, anything that would assure her of his presence. Suddenly I heard a piercing cry. 'You lied, you lied, you lied to me.'

Her crying sobs were mixed with questions and complaints, all full of bitterness. 'Why did you do it?' she cried, knocking on the wall, as if she wanted the wall to answer her. I felt as if my sister's heart was breaking. I wanted to go to her, to hug her, kiss her, tell her how sorry I was. I wanted to cry with her, laugh with her. I wanted to tell her that it was all a vengeful joke, for all the times she wouldn't take me with her. But, I couldn't. My body seemed frozen to the spot where I was standing.

Staggering, I tried to get away from Raya, my head bent down between my shoulders, my eyes blinded by the flowing tears. What started as a prank hurt me as well as my sister.

Three days later we were on the train to Pochep. Raya hardly talked to anyone. Mamma didn't know of the incident. I never lied again, not even for fun.

We arrived in the early evening and walked home from the station. The city had cooled off. A light breeze made walking pleasant.

An Outing

Whenever Mother saw that I felt hurt or offended by my sister she would offer to take me along when she went out.

'Come', she would say, 'we'll visit Aunt Risha and Uncle Leib,' – one of mother's three brothers, he was the only one who lived in Pochep. Mother went to see them at least once a week. She would explain, 'I see them often because, not having any children, they must be lonely.'

They had a food store of all good things to eat, from herring to sweets, even fancy imported chocolate bars. I liked visiting them. While Mamma would go through to their apartment at the back of the store, I would stay behind and inhale all the smells from the foods. I also liked to watch Uncle Leib as he wrapped the items he sold in newspaper.

The floor in the store consisted of loosely connected wooden boards held down by the display of heavy groceries: big sacks of barley, rice and potatoes. At the entrance to the store, Uncle kept big barrels of herring, pickles and sauerkraut. Behind the counter he kept big bags of sugar, salt and an assortment of sweets.

I would watch the customers come in. Uncle Leib's knowledge of what they were asking and how much to charge for it fascinated me.

On this particular visit, Uncle Leib gave me a

chocolate bar to take home. I read on it, 'Imported from Holland'. My knowledge of geography being still limited, I knew only that Holland was not in Russia. It was in Europe, but where exactly I wasn't sure. The chocolate tasted good. I ate half of it. Mother didn't want any. I saved the other half for later.

On the way home we always passed 14 Belaia Street. This time Mother stopped in front of it and said, 'They've finally let this house. Remember, Hannah, how many times we passed it and it was always dark? Now there is a light.'

'Listen, Mamma,' I said. 'There are sounds coming from there . . . beautiful and unfamiliar sounds.'

'It isn't a violin. I heard a blind man playing the violin and people passing dropped coins into his hat,' remembered Mamma, and added, 'It isn't a street organ. I heard a man play one long ago. He had a monkey on top of the organ who danced to the music. I cannot guess what or who is making these sounds.'

What was coming from 14 Balaia Street was pure magic: many sounds at the same time, some sad and melodic, others stormy and demanding. Suddenly, they all melted into a harmonious agreement. I felt frozen to the ground. Mamma spoke as if from a distance. I ran up to the lighted window and pressed my nose to the glass to see better.

In a large-sized room a woman was playing, hitting what looked like a table with white and black keys on it. I asked Mamma to look in. She obliged somewhat unwillingly and pronounced with some pride, 'It is a forte-piano. It comes in different sizes, but this one is surely a big one.'

We went around the house several times to see this wondrous instrument from all sides. In one of the windows I saw a sign: MADAME OLGA SMIRNOVA, GRADUATE OF MOSCOW CONSERVATORY, PIANO TEACHER.

I read it three times, trying to remember each word.

Mamma took my hand and started walking. I felt as if the sounds were following us. I wondered how long I would be able to hear them.

When we returned home the two of us had a quiet dinner. My sister was out visiting and Papa was away on business as usual. I went to sleep, repeating softly, 'Forte-piano, forte-piano.' The next morning I went to my secret friend, the diary, and wrote:

Dear Diary,
I hardly slept last night. When I finally did fall asleep I had a dream in which you came dancing by; half of you looked like one of my school friends with the name 'diary' all over your chest; the other half looked like the instrument we saw and heard last night. You had shining black legs and when you sat down I could play on your thighs. A loud sneeze woke me up. When I fell asleep again, the dream repeated itself, only this time I played on Mamma's thighs and the sounds I produced were awful.

The magical instrument is called forte-piano and the one who will teach anyone to play it is called Olga Smirnova. I want to take lessons. It is still a secret between you and me, until I speak to Mamma. Could the dream mean that Mamma will say no? Oh, please, pray for me, dear Diary.

I found Mamma in the kitchen. She was preparing a meatless soup. It didn't look too promising. Maybe not all of the ingredients were in. I looked at Mamma's face. It didn't look too promising for a serious conversation about lessons on the forte-piano. I was too excited just thinking about it.

'What's missing in the soup, or is it about ready?' I asked, trying not to look at the pot full of grey liquid which was probably going to be our supper.

'A little olive oil, some barley and a few potatoes,'

said Mamma cheerfully, obviously content with her invention. Cautiously I turned the conversation around to the previous evening's outing.

'Mamma,' I said, 'I had a funny dream last night.'

She put the barley in the soup, peeled and cut two potatoes, threw them in, then turned to me and asked, smiling, as if she knew the answer, 'What did you dream about?'

'I dreamed about you, but half of you looked like the forte-piano we saw last night. I could play it by touching the white and black keys which covered your body from the waist down.'

I managed to make Mamma laugh. I saw her face and decided to rush the question. 'Mamma, could I take lessons with Madame Smirnova if it's not too expensive?'

I felt that something should be added, maybe some sacrifice. 'You don't have to get me a new dress for Passover for two years.' I quickly added: 'Not for three or four years.'

I saw that Mamma wanted to say something. I held my breath. 'What good are lessons if you have no way to prepare for them?' she said. 'How will you practise? No piano, and no money to buy one.'

For a minute I was at a loss. Mamma was right. I must give up my dream, for Mamma's lower half was not a forte-piano.

'Don't give up,' I told myself, 'not yet. Think of some way to continue the conversation.'

I heard myself saying, 'Maybe we can find a rich lady who has a piano. She might allow me to practise one hour a day.'

Much to my surprise, my mother took my suggestion seriously. 'If you can find a rich lady with a piano and if you will ask permission to play on her precious instrument, and if you really . . .' She stopped for a moment. I was losing hope, too many 'ifs', but she continued, '. . . if you really will not expect a new dress when your sister is getting one, and if . . .'

'Oh, not another one,' I said softly to myself, trying not to miss any part of the conditions for my dream to come true. I hoped this would be the last 'if'. 'Come on, Mamma,' I whispered.

'Find out how much Madame Smirnova charges. If it's only one rouble, you may take lessons.'

I could hardly believe my ears. My excitement made me sweat. What do I do first? Go to Belaia Street, I told myself.

I ran to number 14 and rang the bell. A woman wearing a loose brown dress opened the door. She had kind dark-brown eyes, brown hair fastened with pins at the back of her neck. She was holding a sheet of music in her hands.

'Yes, little girl, what can I do for you?' she asked.

'I want to learn to play the forte-piano,' I answered fearlessly.

'Although that was its original name, we now call it "piano",' said Madame Smirnova, sounding like a teacher even at the threshold of her house.

She didn't ask me to come in. I was losing my courage. I knew I had to ask her something very important. Stammering, I barely got it out. 'My mother sent me to find out, Madame Smirnova, how much you charge for one lesson a week.'

The teacher looked puzzled. 'Who wants to take the lesson, your mother or you?' she asked.

'It's me,' I said apologetically. 'I heard you playing last night. Do you think I could possibly learn to play like you?'

I immediately realised that it was the wrong thing to say. Madame Smirnova began to laugh. I joined her and the two of us remained at the entrance to her house, obviously amused at such a question.

I felt like saying something. I grabbed her hand and

yelled, 'Madame Smirnova, I know that no one can play like you. I just want to play the forte-piano. Will you teach me even if my mother can only pay a rouble a lesson?'

The teacher suddenly looked very serious. 'How old are you, my dear?'

I quickly answered. 'I'll be eleven in another four months.'

'Yes, I'll teach you,' she said.

Hearing this, I wanted to fly home, but my knees were weak. I managed to ask when I should come for my first lesson. 'Thank you, thank you,' I stammered. 'Do I have to bring any music? What do I have to buy?'

'Just tell me your name and come next Tuesday. I'll get you a beginner's music book.'

I couldn't believe my ears. 'My name is Hannah Kagan. What time on Tuesday?' I rushed these words, and quickly added, 'I'll bring a rouble for the first lesson.'

'I'll see you at two o'clock on Tuesday, Hannah. Goodbye for now.'

I ran all the way home, pushed the *kalitka*[4] open, slammed it closed and got in. The house was empty.

I ran to my diary and wrote in big letters:

WHAT AN IMPORTANT DAY THIS IS. I hear the angels in Heaven singing. They are happy for me. Hannah is now a pupil of Madame Smirnova. She will teach her how to play the forte-piano, which is now called the 'piano'. But her mother is not at home . . . not home, not home to hear the good news . . . to hear the good news. But you, dear Diary, are always here so I can tell you: Tuesday I will sit next to Madame Smirnova and hear and maybe even touch the wondrous keys. I want you to know that this is the first time I went alone to ask for something so important to me.

My sister Raya came home. She asked me, 'Did you
go to see the piano teacher?'

'Yes, I did. She wasn't home.' I wanted Mamma to
hear the good news first. Raya doesn't tell me when
anything special happens to her . . . just because I am
four years younger than she. I was glad to keep something from her.

Mamma got back, carrying a lot of groceries. I ran to
help her and on the way I whispered breathlessly, 'She
took me, Mamma. My first lesson is on Tuesday and I
have to bring a rouble.'

My sister overheard me. 'Why didn't you want me
to know? You are just a child, a sneaky child.'

I pretended that I hadn't heard her and continued
talking to Mamma.

'I have to wait four long days before my first lesson.
Mamma, will you come with me on Tuesday?'

Afraid of hearing her answer, I closed my eyes, but
not my ears, so I couldn't help but hear her say, 'Yes,
I'll come with you. I want to see who charges a whole
rouble just to let you see that a forte-piano has white
and black keys. Even I know that.'

'Mamma, Madame Smirnova will teach me *to play the
piano*, whole melodies,' I answered, trying not to sound
angry. I felt like crying, for even Mamma didn't understand why I had such a strong desire to learn to play
that wondrous instrument.

The First Piano Lesson

I was getting ready, though there were still four days before my first piano lesson on Tuesday. I looked at my hands. The nails seemed too long. With a pair of big scissors I kept cutting them shorter and shorter.

During the weekend, I had made two trips secretly to 14 Belaia Street to make sure that the house, the black piano and the sign were all still there. I read the sign again: MADAME OLGA SMIRNOVA, GRADUATE OF MOSCOW CONSERVATORY, PIANO TEACHER. I could hear the piano again, as I had that late afternoon when mother and I had been returning from a visit with Uncle Leib, and had stopped to listen to the unfamiliar sounds coming from the house.

I had felt special when Madame Smirnova agreed to teach me for a rouble a lesson, the unshakeable condition Mother had insisted on before I went to speak to the piano teacher.

One night I dreamt that when I came for the lesson the teacher took my hand and, instead of leading me to the piano, she hid under it, laughing loudly. I turned around to look for her and began to play, but not with fingers. My buttocks were touching the keys and the sounds they produced were horrible. I woke up crying.

Monday was inspection day. Ears, hair, nails, all were examined for cleanliness. The decision to wear the 'good' dress for the lesson was approved by Mamma. I found the cleanest rouble and put it aside for the teacher.

Tuesday finally arrived. I scrubbed my face and hands several times, and cut my nails a little more out of fear of scratching the beautiful piano.

'Mamma, are you ready?' I asked. 'I mustn't be late.'

'I'll be ready, don't worry. Who do you think Madame Smirnova is?'

'She is a teacher, Mamma, and she has many other pupils like me,' I answered.

After a short walk we were in front of 14 Belaia Street. I was scared. Mamma rang the bell.

'Do you have the rouble?'

'Yes, yes, don't worry,' whispered Mamma. 'Push you hair away from your face. That's better,' she added.

Madame Smirnova was at the door. After introducing herself to Mother she led us to the room with the piano and invited me to sit on the bench in front of it. Mamma was sitting down on a regular chair, close by, but the teacher asked her to wait in the other room. I began to feel dizzy and held my head in my hands to keep it from floating away.

Oh, my poor mother, I thought. She came to *see* how one makes a rouble in a half an hour, not to sit in a dark hall waiting for me.

'Now, let's begin,' said Madame Smirnova, sitting down next to me. Pointing to the piano, she continued, 'This is called a "keyboard". As you can see, it has white and black keys.'

I tried to listen.

'Today you will learn the names of the white keys. They are: doh, ray, me, fah, soh, lah, te, doh.' Madame Smirnova touched the keys as she was naming them. I heard the sounds and felt as if I entered a fairyland.

The teacher and I looked at each other intently. I saw kind dark-brown eyes and a bright blue smock with large white daisies all over it. Madame Smirnova saw in her student an eagerness to learn. She asked, 'Have you heard piano music or any other music before? Pochep is a small town,' she explained apologetically.

'No, never,' I answered quietly, 'only some songs from far away, when I was a small baby. Mamma has told me that they were old revolutionary songs.' That recollection made Madame Smirnova smile.

'I am playing the first scale in C major.' The teacher's voice, competing with the sound, commanded my attention. 'Learn the scale. Play it now. Keep your fingers round and curved.'

She put my right hand on the keyboard. I touched the keys, and as I heard the sounds, my face must have showed disbelief and awe.

Madame Smirnova continued her instruction. 'After using the third finger, put your thumb under and continue with five fingers to finish the scale.'

I followed the instructions and finished playing with the right hand.

Madame Smirnova explained the change that takes place when playing with the left hand. 'Now, try it.'

I was fascinated.

'I'll get you the first book of small simple pieces when you learn to read notes.'

As Madame Smirnova spoke, her fingers kept on playing what to me sounded like a sweet melody and I thought, oh, if I could only sit and listen.

'Do you have a piano at home to practise on?' asked the teacher as she got up. I was afraid to tell the truth, but did.

'No, I don't, but I'll find a way,' I mumbled.

Madame Smirnova wrote down a name and address and handed it to me, saying, 'Tell Mrs Greenberg that I sent you. She is a friend of mine. She will let you practise on her grand piano.'

'Thank you, thank you,' I kept repeating.

'I'll see you next Tuesday,' said the teacher, trying to

stop my mumbling, 'at the same time. Goodbye for now.'

The lesson was over, yet it seemed to me as if it had just begun. I ran to the other room and whispered to Mamma, 'The rouble, the rouble, the lesson is over.'

She put the money in my hand and I ran back to the piano room, the sound of the scale still ringing in my ears.

I was silent. I could tell that Mamma was displeased. She probably thought that the scale I had kept repeating wasn't worth a rouble. 'What else did she teach you?' asked Mother.

All I could say was, 'Didn't you hear her play that nice little melody?' I knew what the answer would be – what melody? But for me, the lesson had only one fault: it was too short.

Mother walked ahead of me. I had to run to catch up with her. When I did, I got hold of her skirt to make sure I could see and hear her. 'Mamma, the teacher gave me the name of her friend who has a piano. She wrote down her name and address. Here it is.'

Mother looked at the note and in a soft voice responded, 'I know who she is. She lives not far from us, but you will have to go alone to see her about practising.'

'Why, Mother? Why won't you come with me?'

'Because, I don't like to go begging for favours. If I have no piano, I don't try to play one.'

I had another 'floating away' spell. I had never been too far alone as yet, except once to a nearby farm for a container of milk. Still, two days later, I put on my good dress again and walked over to the big apartment house with large black doors and big grey windows.

I pressed the doorbell where the sign said GREENBERG. The door opened. A nice-looking blonde woman in a tight black dress greeted me. She took the note I had brought and invited me to come in. I followed her.

The shining black piano made everything in the room look expensive. The blue velvet sofa, the small chairs with their silk covers, seemed to be there just to make the piano look grander. Seeing these luxurious pieces of furniture made me suddenly realise why Mother had said to me, 'You will have to go alone'. She knew that to see a house with a big, good-looking black piano, like the one that Madame Smirnova had, meant to see a rich house. Returning to her own house would make her sad, and she wanted to avoid this.

Mrs Greenberg showed me the piano and said I was welcome to practise on it. 'You see, Hannah,' she explained, 'I bought the piano for my daughter who is about your age, but she doesn't show any interest in it. Maybe when she hears you play she might change her mind.'

We agreed that I should come three times a week to practise and that the time would be specified by Mrs Greenberg each week.

When I got back, my sister was home. She greeted me with 'Hannah and her piano, which she hasn't got.' This became a daily joke in the family circle. At first I smiled every time I heard it. Just the mention of the word 'piano' made me feel good and warm inside. But as the weeks passed I began to feel more and more the meaning of Mother's 'You will have to go alone.'

The diary became my only friend, where I secretly expressed my thoughts and feelings about music without being scolded or laughed at. I would pass my sister without stopping, and run to the other room to write down what I saw, heard and felt.

Oh, dear, dear Diary
I've just returned from Mrs Greenberg's.

She must feel very happy – she has a *piano*. But, she has no one to play it. Is there one who decides these things? Why is there nobody in my family who even likes the piano? I now go for my lesson earlier (but no one knows it), so that I can sit and listen to students who can really play.

It has become such an important voice in my life, but I can tell this only to you. All I hear at home is, 'You will have to go alone'. And I am walking away, running away from home, home, home. Oh, here comes Mamma. I have to stop for now.

A Trip

'My name is Hannah Kagan.'
'Where are you going?'
'I am going to Balaklava Station to visit my Aunt Tzippah Chaykin.'

This was rehearsal number three. Mamma asked the questions and I had to give the right answers. She was preparing me for the first trip I would take alone. I was scared. I even asked Mamma why I had to go. A long explanation followed: 'You were a sick little girl, remember? You had a bad cough. Now you have to eat well, gain strength. My sister Tzippah has very good food and she has invited you for a short vacation. School is finished for the holidays. Before it gets too hot, you go.'

As if to reassure me, Mother added, 'You'll meet her two sons, one from the first marriage, the other from her present husband. They are just a little older than you.'

I listened to her and got more and more excited about the trip. At night, before falling asleep, I heard train whistles which made me think of far-away places.

'So, what's your name?' Mamma didn't trust my memory.

'Please, I know everything by heart.'

She finally gave up. 'We'll pack tomorrow.' Mother sounded tired.

What would I have to take? A good dress, of course. Before Passover my sister and I would get new dresses. That usually took several trips. We were allowed to go with Mother, first to a few fabric stores to compare quality and prices. Mother would ask the owner of each store, 'How durable is this material? Will it withstand rough handling? Is this the last price, or can you make it less expensive?'

At that point my sister and I would step away, pretending to look at other goods. I loved the smell of material so I always had a good time in the store. When Mother had decided which lucky merchant would get her purchase we would visit his store again. We were also allowed to choose buttons for our new dresses. The last time I had picked a big pearl-like one.

I liked to look at the endless shelves of small boxes, each with its own button glued to the front of it. I thought every box contained a secret. If you opened the right one, the contents of it would make you rich or famous, maybe even both.

The next step in getting a new dress a year was the trip to the dressmaker – the same big, cheerful seamstress we had been going to for the last five years. Irina Ivanovna was her name. I liked to hear her say, when she took our measurements: 'Sleeve, thirteen centimetres; length, thirty.' When she said it, it sounded different for she mispronounced certain letters. It was funny, but we wouldn't laugh. Three trips (the second for a fitting and the third for a triumphant completion of her labour), and the two of us owned new dresses.

This year, though I still went with Mamma and Raya to the stores and the dressmaker, I only looked and smelled the fabrics while they were choosing material and buttons for Raya's dress, hoping that some day I would join Raya again in picking and choosing materials and buttons.

Mother looked at me sadly and whispered, 'Maybe

next spring, if I have the money, you will not give up a new dress because you are taking piano lessons.'

Finally, the day to pack my things arrived. Mother and I had a long discussion as to what an eleven-year-old girl should take along for a two-week vacation. I only had Raya's good dress of two years ago, made over for me. So we decided that I would wear the everyday dress, and the good one I would carry, plus a change of underwear and a toothbrush.

'But how will I carry it all?' I asked.

'In a big kerchief,' said Mother. I felt sorry not to have a suitcase, but when we got to the station I saw that most passengers carried similar bundles.

Mother bought my ticket while I listened to the whistles and watched the trains come and go, each one full of promise.

She gave me the ticket, with last minute instructions to remember where I was going and what my name was. 'Here is a piece of bread and an apple in case you get hungry,' she said. 'Aunt Tzippah will meet you at the station. It only takes five hours. I'd better go now.' She kissed me goodbye.

I didn't want to be left alone before the train arrived. I felt like crying out, 'Mamma, wait, I have to say something to you . . . I am not afraid, but . . .' It was on my tongue but tears were choking me. Mamma was gone. I ran to a bench. My knees gave way. Somebody tried to help me.

'Come on, little girl, sit down.' The train arrived with a lot of steam and a loud whistle. The conductor helped me to find a seat.

I closed my eyes and went through the day before my departure. Poor Mother was alone now. My sister had left earlier to see a friend. Being fifteen, she thought herself grown up. She had said, 'So long, send me a card.' Father was away on business, as usual.

My thoughts switched to my Aunt Tzippah and her

family: boys, two of them, both older than I. It would probably be best to stay away from them.

I looked out the window of the train. We were passing forests, small villages and some railway stations, but the train did not stop. I saw some passengers eating and remembered my bread and apple. They tasted better than usual. I listened to the sound of the wheels as they glided over the tracks . . . steady, steady, on ahead, faster, faster. Slower, slower, slower, stop.

Two stops more before we got to Balaklava. Some of the passengers ran out and came back with containers of steaming hot water which they drank as if it were tea. I was falling asleep when the conductor touched my shoulder gently to remind me that the next stop was mine. I shook off the crumbs from my snack, tied my little bundle and watched the train come to a full stop.

I saw a woman outside looking at every window of the train. It could be my Aunt Tzippah. I stepped down the three high steps and ran straight into her arms. It felt good not to be alone any more. The boys were not with her. How lucky.

Aunt Tzippah looked tall, strong and very sure of herself. Her house was big. I liked everything about it: the new, shining floors, the many windows and the smell of pine trees coming from the forest surrounding it. Aunt Tzippah told me it was built especially for them when her husband took the job of supervising the station. She was proud of the house.

I met my cousins, Ziama and Aaron. They looked at me as if to say, 'A girl, what can we expect?' All four of us stood and waited. For what? Aunt Tzippah went to the kitchen, followed by Aaron. Ziama and I were left alone. Finally he asked me, 'How was the trip?'

I rushed my answer. 'Just fine. I love trains. It was too short. I looked out of the window all the time.' I didn't know what else to say. I wanted to sound intelligent but my cousin looked bored. Aunt Tzippah called me. I felt relieved.

'Hannah, are you hungry?'

'No,' I answered, but quickly added, 'but I want to see your kitchen.' I found my way to it through a maze of little halls, big doors and open cupboards.

'What a nice kitchen,' I said. A big stove was on one side of the kitchen. A round table stood in the middle with six chairs hugging it. The floors were the same shining wooden ones as in the other rooms. All of them must enjoy eating here. Who wouldn't? It was pleasant, cheerful and warm.

My aunt showed me to my room. It had a window, a desk with a chair, and a small bed. I felt very special. At home, the room where I slept looked more like a cupboard in comparison – it had no window and no door.

Sleep didn't come. Too much to think about. The whistles of passing trains made me feel closer to home. I woke up from a bad dream, hours later: my mother flew in through a window and wanted to take me home. 'This is no place for you . . . too many things are new for you here.' I begged her to let me stay a little longer. She refused.

Aunt Tzippah was standing over me. 'Get up, Hannah, breakfast is ready.' It felt good to be a guest. I got washed and dressed in a hurry, following Mother's instructions: 'Good dress only for going out.'

The light was bright, the sun was warm. Aunt Tzippah's family were all sitting around the table. The food smelled good, a big Russian breakfast: boiled potatoes, steaming hot, sliced herring on a big platter, black bread, butter, cottage cheese, and hot cocoa for the young ones, tea for the others. I ate much more than I did at home. Everything tasted so good. Aunt Tzippah stood over me, refilling my plate. I liked the attention as well as the food.

The days were filled with pleasant things. On the third day a boy named David came to see Aaron and Ziama. They were students at the same college. David suggested a walk. To my surprise, I was invited to join them. Aunt Tzippah must have told them to take me along.

I disappeared for a few minutes to change into my good dress. I was excited and jittery. My feet hardly touched the ground. Three boys and me!

They hardly noticed me. I was there only because Aunt Tzippah had arranged it. I tried to listen to their conversation. They talked of books. They were very serious. But the air felt good and I enjoyed wearing the good dress even though I remembered the make-over procedure from Raya to me. The passing trains sang their inviting song. We got back two hours later and I was glad I had gone.

The walks became our daily exercise, with or without David. We walked along the railway tracks where the sand and pebbles crunched under our feet. We returned as the sun began to dip below the horizon. A hot dinner would be waiting for us.

My cousins were getting used to my presence, as an unavoidable nuisance. Much to my surprise, during one of our outings when they were discussing Karl Marx and Engels, Aaron turned to me and asked, 'Hannah, have you read *Das Kapital* by Karl Marx?'

Oh, God. What should I say? If I lied and said yes, further questions would get me into more trouble. If I told the truth and said no, they would give up on me and blame it all on the fact that I was a girl. And just when I was beginning to enjoy our walks.

'Dialectical materialism is the struggle of opposites,' said Aaron.

'Karl Marx was dependent on Engels for financial aid,' said Ziama.

Aaron repeated the question. 'Well, have you or have you not read *Das Kapital*?'

I decided to tell the truth. 'No, I have not read *Das Kapital* as yet, but I promise to read it this summer.'

They looked at me, first shocked, then amused. I was encouraged to continue: 'I am learning a lot from you and I will try to remember that Friedrich Engels and Marx collaborated on the *Communist Manifesto*. When Karl Marx went to Paris to live, his association with Engels began.'

I thought my memory had impressed them but I still felt ashamed to have understood so little of their discussion.

The two weeks passed very quickly. I said goodbye to the boys. They looked at me sternly and said, 'We trust you, don't forget, keep your promise.'

Aunt Tzippah took me to the station where she would also meet her husband, who was returning from a business trip. I carried my little bundle. Aunt Tzippah put a few goodies in it for me to munch on the train. During the five hours on the train I watched, regretfully, the pine trees disappearing. The train came to a stop. My station – Pochep.

I was glad to see the familiar face of my mother. Mother kissed me. I hugged her. Not used to such a demonstration of affection, I turned to see if anyone was looking. We walked out of the station, which looked grey and deserted. Mamma told me I looked healthier. She asked me about the visit. I wanted to talk about what I remembered best: how much good food there was to eat every day and how I loved the smell of the pine trees. I wanted to tell her what we had for breakfast every day, but she suddenly squeezed my hand and asked, 'How can you talk so much about food? Tell me better, did you like Aunt Tzippah?'

'I liked her very much,' I answered and added, 'also my cousins Ziama and Aaron.'

Mamma smiled as if I had said something she hadn't expected to hear. She always had that mysterious smile whenever I mentioned anything about boys.

I knew that the two weeks spent in Balaklava were a part of me now: the smell of pine trees after an early summer rain, and the awakened desire to know as much as my cousins did would stay with me for ever. Still *Das Kapital* scared me a little. Should I keep my promise to read it? Would I understand it?

I didn't tell Mamma about my walks with the boys, nor about the Karl Marx incident. I decided to keep this a secret, which would need a special time and place to talk about.

Grandpa's Visit

When I returned from Balaklava, I noticed how small our house looked in the courtyard after Aunt Tzippah's big house with a room for every member of the family and large pine trees guarding it.

'How are Raya and Papa?' I asked Mamma. Her answer was short: 'Your sister Raya went to see a friend. She'll be home later. Papa is out of town on business.'

When we got home, Mother offered me something to eat. I looked at the plate of pickled cabbage and tomatoes. 'I don't feel hungry enough, Mamma,' I said quietly.

'Then have a glass of milk,' insisted Mamma, as she poured a glass of tea for herself and a smaller one of milk for me. It felt good to be home alone with Mother.

'I got a letter from Grandpa,' she informed me. 'He is coming to stay with us for a while.'

'When, Mamma, when is he coming?' I asked eagerly. She answered with a sigh, 'A week from tomorrow, at four in the afternoon.'

Of four grandparents, Grandpa, my mother's father, was the only one alive.

'Where is he going to sleep?' I asked.

'That's what I would like to know,' Mother answered.

I would have offered him my bed if I had had one. I slept on a trunk in the small room.

After a lot of discussion, it was decided finally that

Grandpa would sleep in the eating-room. Two chairs would be added to a bench, with some blankets for softness on top.

Mamma explained why she had selected that room. 'Grandpa probably gets up early,' she said, 'as all old people do, so it won't bother him if the room is used for eating as well as for sleeping.'

A few days before his arrival, Mother called Raya and me and said, 'Girls, I think you should know something about your grandfather, now that you will be meeting him for the first time. When I was growing up, I saw very little of him. He had to serve as a soldier in the army for twenty-five years. This *ukase*, or rule, was signed by Tzar Nicholas I, to be obeyed by Jews who failed to pay taxes, or who had no money to bribe the officials. Father was allowed to visit his family for short periods several times a year.'

'Did the army pay Grandpa?' asked Raya.

'Yes,' answered Mamma, 'but very little. We had a small sweet shop that my mother ran while taking care of her family, which grew bigger every two years. Of six children, I was the youngest.'

I ran over to Mother, put my hands on her shoulders and burst out, 'Oh, Mamma, you must have had a hard life.' Mother covered my hands with hers and whispered, 'Yes, Hannah, I did.'

In the evening, after we all had had some barley soup with bread, I went to my corner where the trunk on which I slept served me also as a table, and opening the cheerful red covers, I wrote:

Dear Diary, my secret friend,
Here I am. I have a lot to tell you. Here is what took place recently. After a winter of bronchitis, Mother sent me to her sister, Tzippah, to eat better, sleep more and get healthier. Yes, I went alone, for the first time. When I came back everything looked and felt

different. Aunt Tzippah had more of everything, more food, more rooms, more good-smelling pine trees and more boys than I have seen in all my eleven years of life. And I liked the boys, but the books they had been talking about, like *Das Kapital*, I am afraid, were too grown up for me. Still, I promised them to read it. Now, the biggest news: Grandpa is coming. Mamma told us he is seventy years old and he spent twenty-five years of his life in the army. So, I have a project: how to make every day of Grandpa's visit special. I have to think, and think hard.

Four days before Grandpa's arrival, our Hebrew teacher, Chayca, came in the afternoon to give us a lesson. When we sat down at the table in the eating-room, we told her that Grandpa was coming. She wanted to know something about him, but neither I nor my sister could satisfy her curiosity.

'Do you know how old your grandfather is?' asked Chayca.

'Yes, that's one thing we do know. He is seventy years old,' I answered.

She didn't tell us what she had in mind, but when she came for our second lesson that week, she brought a book with her. 'I was glad to have found this book written in Russian by a man called Dubnov,' she said. 'It tells you a little bit about the life of Jews in your grandfather's time. Read the chapter "Military Despotism of Nicholas I".'

Raya read it aloud. I was glad to have this information, which verified what Mother had told us.

On Monday, one day before Grandpa's arrival, Chayca came to give us what was to be the last lesson. Mamma had to stop them for lack of money. She came in. Her black wavy hair was brushed back and caught in a bun. She wore the same white blouse, black skirt and high-laced shoes, and her young face looked as if it had just been scrubbed.

The lesson started in the usual way. We were sitting at the big round table. As I read from the Book of Prophets, I noticed something moving on top of the teacher's head. I looked up and saw a big, well-fed louse. It moved as if it knew all the exits and entrances of its habitat. It behaved like a permanent tenant on Chayca's head.

When Raya took over the reading, I was so busy watching the louse that I didn't hear a word. During that hour my sister learned more than I, but Chayca never knew that a louse occupied my attention. In concentrating on the unwelcome tenant on Chayca's head, I had a rest from planning the project of getting to know Grandpa.

Grandpa arrived when expected. I wanted to meet him at the station, but Mother thought it best for Raya and me to wait for him at home.

When he came in I stretched my arms out for a hug but didn't even get to shake hands with him. He just said, 'Hello, little one.'

I started to say, 'I am so glad you ...', but he walked away and didn't hear me.

He looked tall with his long white beard. His face was pale, his body thin, and his blue eyes small, as if he were afraid to see too much. He wore a long black coat which he used in the house as a jacket.

Grandpa spoke Yiddish most of the time. I ran after him, according to the planned project and asked, 'Are you hungry, Grandpa, would you like something to eat, or maybe a glass of tea?'

He looked at me, an attempt of a smile lighting his face as he answered, 'No, no, my child.'

I gave it another try: 'Would you like to sit down in the other room on a couch? It is softer than a chair.'

I took his hand to lead him to the other room. He

withdrew his hand but followed me. Raya joined us. The three of us went to the sitting-room. Mother got busy preparing the evening meal. My sister looked undisturbed by the silence. I persevered.

'How was the trip, Grandpa, easy, pleasant or long?' I gave him a choice, hoping to get an answer.

'It was pleasant,' I heard him say. Then, in Yiddish, *'Ich bin mit.'* (I understood it to mean 'I am tired.')

I went to the kitchen and said to Mamma that Grandpa was tired, maybe we could eat earlier so that he could go to rest after supper. Mother agreed.

We had a thick potato soup, black bread and a prune compote. Grandpa ate well, hardly talked, but listened to us talk. After some lengthy preparations, we went to bed.

The following morning I got up early enough to help Grandpa wash his face and hands. But when I went to the kitchen to see him, he was dressed and looking at the courtyard, obviously ready for breakfast, or at least some tea. Mother was out, probably getting some provisions. My sister Raya was still asleep.

'Hello, Grandpa, did you sleep well?' I yelled, for fear he couldn't hear me.

He turned around, walked toward me, and without a smile said, 'Yes, yes, where is your mother?'

Though I did not know exactly where she was, I said, 'She'll be home soon. What would you like to do today?'

He looked surprised at the question and didn't answer. I tried again, 'Would you like me to take you for a walk?'

'No, no,' was his answer.

'Grandpa, how would you like to go to the public baths?'

'That wouldn't be bad.' His words came out faster.

'I'll take you tomorrow,' I promised.

I had obviously touched upon something familiar to Grandpa, as well as pleasurable; I could have jumped for joy. What a happy turn for me. 'Hang on to it,' I said to myself, 'don't lose it.' For me, the first public baths trip had been a memorable experience, seeing so many nude women of all shapes and sizes for the first time. But I remember feeling uncomfortable and wanting to get out of there.

The next day I told Mother about it. She gave me detailed directions as to how to get there, and supplied Grandpa with a towel and a bar of soap. At four in the afternoon we were on our way. When we got close enough, I told Grandpa that I would wait for him here, sitting down on the first bench I saw.

An hour later Grandpa came out, his face red but visibly relaxed.

'Was it good and hot?' I asked Grandpa.

'It was very good and very hot,' he answered.

I wanted to ask him so many questions but still felt that the time was not right. I did take his hand in mine and we walked home, hand in hand. I felt pleased with my project so far.

At supper time, I moved the better pieces of meat to his side whenever Mamma wasn't looking, though she was attentive enough. Still, I saw some disapproval on her face occasionally.

I began to plan the next excursion. Should I take Grandpa to the synagogue or would he rather see where the rich people lived in Pochep? The rich neighbourhood won. It was closer and, as little as I knew of Grandpa, I decided that he would enjoy it.

One day Mamma sent Grandpa on an errand. It was a bright, early summer morning. After a skimpy breakfast, I began my cleaning chores. This was the day for scrubbing floors. Just as I was putting old white towels on the damp kitchen floor to walk on, Grandpa returned. He quietly and carefully stepped over the dry spots and went into the eating-room. When Mother saw him she followed him there. In a little while, I heard screams, yells and cries coming from the room. I ran to see what had happened. They were arguing, but not in Russian.

Little by little, I found out that Mamma had sent Grandpa to the post office with twenty-five roubles to post to Papa who had to pay for a business purchase. Between sobs and tears, Grandpa tried to tell Mother what had happened. He said he had wanted to see if the money was securely in his pocket, but then he had switched pockets, forgetting that the second one had a big hole in it. Grandpa had lost the money. Both of them were crying now.

'I shouldn't have trusted you with the money,' yelled Mamma.

I left to finish scrubbing the kitchen floor, but I couldn't stay away. When I returned, I saw Grandpa sitting in a chair, holding his head in his hands. Mother was standing in the corner, blowing her nose. Her eyes were red and wet. When she saw me she left the room abruptly.

Grandpa was rocking back and forth, his eyes were closed. He mumbled quietly, as if he were praying . . . most of it in Russian.

'I was afraid . . . afraid to tell you about the money.' Grandpa didn't know that Mamma had left the room. He kept on talking to himself, between loud, heavy moaning. Tears were running down his cheeks.

'I remember,' he went on, rocking himself as he spoke, 'I still remember your anger. Oh, how angry you got when . . . still a child, too young for anger, you had to care for all your brothers and sisters when your mother died.' He stopped talking to wipe his tears and blow his nose, but the rocking didn't stop. I wanted to ask Mother, 'Were you really angry? Were you the youngest and had to work so hard? What about the others?' But she was too upset to answer questions of so long ago.

I went over to Grandpa and took his hand in mine. He opened his eyes, looked at me, but pulled his hand back as if he wanted to say 'Don't pity me'.

The day ended. Raya was out most of the day and missed it all. Mother called: 'Tea is ready.' No one answered her call. The heavy rain outside suited the mood inside. We all went to bed.

The following morning when I went to the kitchen to help Mother with the breakfast dishes, she told me that Grandpa would be leaving the next day to visit Chaya-Esther. The only Grandpa I had, and he was going away. *Maybe I'll never see him again*. That's what I thought, but didn't say. I followed him around. Maybe he'd ask me, 'Why are you at my side so much, my child?', and then I could tell him, 'I don't want you to leave, Grandpa, not now, after I have got to know you.' I couldn't answer questions he never asked.

The next day when I woke up I heard Mamma talking to her father. 'You'd better eat something, Father, you'll be on the train most of the day.'

All was quiet. Grandpa didn't answer.

'I am talking to you, Papa.' She sounded too strict. Why did Mother speak so sternly to Grandpa on the day of his going away? I asked myself. And my sister, Raya, also gave him up.

'Oh, Grandpa,' I whispered, with a sigh.

Mamma was getting ready to take Grandpa to the station. He had brought nothing with him, so he had nothing to take, not even a bundle.

To say goodbye, Grandpa walked over to face me, closed his eyes and kissed me on the forehead. I touched his black coat and looked at him with tears in my eyes.

Suddenly, he took both my hands in his and told me quietly in Russian, 'Your mother was a little girl like you when I left for the army. Now, I see her again; she is a mother and you are the little girl.'

'Father, we have to go if you want to catch the train.'

He turned around and followed Mother to the door.
I remained standing, trying to remember what
Grandpa had said. Something was stirring in Grandpa's
old heart. He hadn't lived long enough with us to tell
us what it was.

Father – A Guest in the House

Dear Diary,

I'll let you in on a secret about my father. I love to be near him. It must be wrong, or else why would I want to keep it a secret? He smells of far-away places. When I open his suitcase, I see things we don't have in the house: hairbrushes with fancy handles, special bags for ties, for underwear. If I look soon after he returns, I find several bars of chocolate and even some oranges.

Maybe he leads a double life. He is the great merchant when he is away from home. Perhaps that's why he often has no money for the family. When he is here, he expects all three of us to take care of him, especially when he is sick and needs a doctor or a fancy diet that he believes will cure him.

I remember, healthy or sick, poorer or richer, the best and the most nourishing tidbits go to Papa, even if it means that the three of us will eat less that day. And yet, in spite of it, or maybe because of it, I feel it is a holiday whenever he is home. Well, DD, I have to stop sharing my thoughts with you and see if Mother needs my help.

Papa, even the word – Papa – was special to me. He travelled a lot, was at home very little. When he did come home he'd always be dressed well and smell good.

At meals he was treated as a guest, for he would either be recovering from an illness or complaining of one.

When the dinner included meat, he had chicken. If the meal was what Mamma called *paravay*[5], or if the meal were meatless, Papa would be served various cheese delicacies, which we couldn't touch.

I wouldn't speak to my father unless he spoke to me first. Yet whenever he looked at me I could see a warm gleam in his eyes, as if he wanted to say, 'You are a nice little girl as long as you leave me alone.' When he was near my sister, Raya, he would look cold and uninterested. At Mamma, he hardly looked at all. Still, Mother tried to please him.

In the mornings, I'd listen to the song my mother sang. If it was a happy song, it meant Mamma had no argument with father. Most of the time the songs were sad and made me cry. I tried to guess what they were arguing about. One time I overheard them – the argument was about money.

I remember Papa coming home for Passover – an important Jewish holiday. He would return from the synagogue ... everything had to be ready for the ritual of the Seder. Everyone had to be sitting at the table. Since I was the youngest, I had to ask the four questions, to remind ourselves and the world why we celebrate Passover. Once, I remember being late for the first Seder. I was scolded severely. Papa's anger didn't go away. I didn't ask the four questions any more, and neither did anyone else. At every Seder we had to eat bitter things, such as horseradish, symbolic of enslavement; and sweet things, such as apples, in memory of being freed. Every time I thought of that angry Seder, I'd cry myself to sleep.

Sometimes Papa would be home for Rosh Hashanah, the Jewish New Year. He would then bring oranges, apples and lemons. It felt good to taste fresh fruit so late in the season – something we couldn't get in our small store.

Little by little I found out why Papa was away from home so much, and why the family was short of money so often. Papa was a fur tanner. His income depended on the peasants whose profession was hunting. They sold the skins of the animals to Papa, who had a list of furriers, buyers of these skins. The furriers would take the skins to their own workshops to make them soft and ready for fur coats. Mamma explained it to me one rainy afternoon. The reason we were short of money, Mamma said, was due to the fact that the peasants got drunk and the hunting had to wait until they were sober.

When Papa came home sick it was a bad time for all of us. My sister and I would have to go for the doctor. Sometimes we went together to the doctor's office to ask the doctor to come to see Papa. He lived not far away but in a better neighbourhood, full of flowers in the spring and colourful young trees in the autumn. The doctor, or, if he wasn't there, a woman, would take the address and give us an approximate time when the doctor could see Papa.

During Father's frequent battles with illness, our lives would be devoted exclusively to his needs, with the intrusion of an important stranger – the doctor. He became a kind of diversion for me as well as an angel of hope.

Before the doctor's arrival the house got a thorough cleaning. Some things that had no special place were put away. Very often no one remembered where to look for them. The right amount of money was prepared to avoid confusion when the doctor had to be paid.

Then there was Papa's diet. It usually contained more expensive cuts of meat, or fresh dairy products, that Mamma wouldn't buy for us. All of us were making every effort to get Papa well as quickly as possible.

When the doctor arrived we knew it even before he

entered. His knock was most insistent, as if he were saying, 'Open the door at once, if you know who is here.' Mamma, my sister and I stood around the doctor and watched his every move, as though he were a magician, or at least an assistant to God. He usually gave orders to the patient or to us: 'Open the window, close the door, cover him, turn him over', all of it said in a commanding voice that each of us obeyed. Papa seemed to get better just because the doctor was there. Before we knew it, the doctor would have finished the examination. He would write a prescription for medication, but we still wouldn't know what was wrong with Papa.

When the doctor was ready to leave, I'd watch him closely, to see how the money the doctor received would get to his pocket. Money changed hands in such a way that it remained a secret between the one who gave and the one who received. Maybe the doctor was ashamed to be paid for his work since, next to God, he was the only one who could help the patient to get well.

Mamma kept the two roubles in her hand. As she said goodbye to the doctor, they shook hands. The two roubles were transferred to the doctor's hand, and he immediately put them in his pocket. The procedure remained known only to Mamma and the doctor. I would look to see if the money missed the pocket and hit the floor. The doctor must have practised that exchange a lot, for the money disappeared into the pocket every time.

I started writing the diary, I think, mostly because I wanted to put down on paper what I felt about my father. I knew he was my father, but I didn't quite know what part a father plays when he is a Papa in the family. As time went on, and I wasn't a baby any more, I often felt that he was a stranger to be admired and feared at the same time. The diary gradually became my invisible friend, in front of whom I wasn't afraid to be wrong, ashamed or in doubt. It was in the diary that I asked questions – for many of which I had no answers. One of the most bothersome, unanswerable questions that appeared again and again was why Mother sounded unhappy most of the time. Was it a lack of money or, maybe, Papa's absence from home? I would think to myself that Papa didn't know how to be a father, or a husband. Affection – I saw more of it in the families of our relatives when we visited them.

I Miss Mother

I remember Mamma getting sick only once. When she had a headache, she would remain in bed and ask one of us to stay at home. But this time was different. When my sister and I returned from school, the door from the other room opened and at the threshold stood Mamma in a beautiful brown coat and brown hat, looking very important. She obviously wanted to surprise us, for the said, 'I am going to Gomel, a nice big town not far from here.'

My sister and I cried out: 'Whatever for?'

'To get well,' came back a fast reply. 'There is a good doctor,' continued Mamma, 'who does operations, and he'll help me to get well.'

I wanted to know what Mother's illness was but didn't dare ask. I thought it was brave of Mamma to stay away from home at a time like this. When Mamma came over to me and kissed me goodbye, I began to cry. Mamma hugged me and said: 'Your sister is a big girl; she'll take good care of you.' Before she left, she mentioned that Papa would meet her in Gomel. I was glad that she wouldn't be alone.

Suddenly the house was empty. Raya was already in the kitchen preparing something for our evening meal, taking her new responsibilities seriously.

The first night was a little scary but also exciting for

the two of us to be alone. I was allowed to sleep in Mother's big bed.

The next day Aunt Brocha came and said, 'I've brought you some cooked food that I know you like.'

I missed Mamma. I always thought she came with a house and a Papa. Thinking about family helped me pretend Mamma was still at home.

My sister came in to wake me up. 'Get up, Hannah! We'll be late for school.' She sounded excited. 'Hurry!' she added.

'Oh, Raya, I had a strange dream. Papa's family, Mamma's family, all came to see Mamma but we couldn't find her. Where is Mamma? I am worried about her! Maybe she is sick, Raya. I miss Mamma . . .' I started to cry. My sister ran over to me with a hairbrush in her hand and said, 'Come on, Hannah, let's have breakfast. Mamma will be back soon.' She began brushing my hair. I was surprised. How did Raya know that Mamma did just that when she wanted to make me feel better? She must have watched Mother doing it more than once. Her brushing strokes were gentle and precise. It felt good. I wiped my eyes and tried to stop crying. I asked Raya, 'Will you know how to be a mamma?' She laughed but didn't answer.

That day we ate the food Aunt Brocha brought and it was good. The following day Raya made a kind of stew that I had never eaten before. I tasted it and said, 'Somehow, I am not hungry today. I must have eaten too much yesterday.' I hoped she believed me. My sister tried so hard. I didn't want to hurt her.

I was counting the days. Mother said she would be back in a week. Three more days left. Several times I caught myself speaking to Mother, forgetting that she wasn't there. It made me sad. 'Mamma, where are you? I miss you. Come back! Hurry up! Get well and come back.' I closed my eyes and tried to picture the place where Mother would be now. Was it a hotel? No. It couldn't be a hotel. Most likely a hospital. What does a hospital look like? I had never seen one. Maybe she was lying in a bed, waiting for a doctor to come.

'Oh, Mamma, come back. I don't like my sister's cooking and I have to talk to you about so many things.'

I remembered the time when I went to Aunt Tzippah. I was afraid then, too. But that was only for a few hours; then, my aunt became Mamma for two weeks. But Raya couldn't be a mamma yet; that must be why I was so lonely, wishing for my mother to be here.

Mamma kept her promise. She came home in a week and she seemed to be well again.

Sonia Greenberg's Room

Dear D,

Many things are happening. First: Papa was sick –
that's really not new. This time it took him longer to
recover. The doctor keeps telling us what his sickness
is called, but I cannot remember it. Mamma went to
another city to get well. She had an operation. I know
that an operation is performed when something has
to be taken out, but Mamma didn't tell us everything.
She is back and I am glad. Raya tried to take care of
everything, but I still missed Mamma. My piano lessons are getting harder to learn, and practising at the
Greenbergs' is not always pleasant.

Last time I went there Sonia invited me to her
room. I think she wanted me to see how rich she is.
Her bed, as well as three shelves on the wall, were all
full of dolls – big dolls, little dolls, dolls with open
eyes, dolls with closed eyes, gypsy dolls, dolls dressed
in costumes from strange lands, boy dolls in peasant
embroidered shirts, dolls in tutus, even baby dolls!

When Sonia saw my bewilderment in the way I
was running from one doll to another, she asked me
'Haven't you ever seen dolls before? Don't you have
any dolls of your own?'

She looked surprised to hear me say, 'No. I've
never seen any dolls before.'

'Where do you buy these dolls?' I asked Sonia.

'In a toy store,' she answered.

'What is a toy store?'

Sonia laughed before answering.

You know, DD, I am ashamed. Is it possible that I am the only one who has never been to a toy store? Am I the only one who has not had any dolls, or any toys?

DD, I am writing down a lot of questions in need of answers, to find out if one answer that I found a long time ago is right. When I was seven years old, a family who lived three houses away from us had a little girl the same age. Every time a maid took her out for a walk, she wore a dark-blue winter coat with an ermine collar.

Every time I saw her go out, I would stand at the *kalitka* of our yard to watch her parade in her ermine-trimmed coat. One day I asked Mother about the family of the little girl and Mamma told me that her father was a lawyer. I decided then and there that when I grow up I will be a lawyer and have a coat with an ermine collar.

So here, DD, are my questions: who decides how big a house should be? When they have children, is it too late to ask for a change in the decision? Why do I have to wait 'til I become a lawyer to have an ermine collar on my coat? Why cannot my Papa buy one for me now? Why does my Aunt Tzippah have a nicer house than we have and better food to eat?

Now, I'll tell you some of my answers to these questions. Everybody has to pay for everything they want to have. Mamma paid for my ticket before I could get on a train to visit Aunt Tzippah. When I go to the market with Mamma, I see that some foods cost less, others cost more. Mamma buys what she can for the money she has. *Money is the big answer*.

Is learning also for sale? Not for me. I love it for its own sake. In school there is more to learn. We

have one new teacher in addition to Elisaveta
Petrovna. Her name is Vera Ivanovna. She has dark
eyes and black hair. Her olive skin is soft. Her smile is
kind. She teaches maths – the beginning of it, algebra –
all about axioms and theorems.

I like Vera Ivanovna; she explains willingly and
enjoys the class. I want to be her favourite pupil.
Now, I have found two things that have a special
order about them: the composer Bach on the piano
with his little minuets and gavottes, and algebra in
school. I think and I learn.

As I write down my thoughts in my secret diary, I
feel that I am doing it for the first time. Yet I know
that I have been doing it for several years. It helps
me to sort things out about money, learning and
family. There seems to be a connection between all
three. Families are related, yet money and learning
are distributed unevenly among them.

My parents' families are large on both sides. And
that's no secret. I needn't hide them in my diary.
Mama has three brothers and two sisters. Papa has
one sister and three brothers. Only two of my uncles
live not far from us. One uncle has a store and he is
the one who wraps herring in newspaper. The other
uncle like my father is a fur tanner. His name is Leivik
and his wife is my Aunt Brocha.

I love the visits to this aunt; she has a bigger house
than ours. There is always someone helping her with
her household chores, maybe because she has three
sons and no daughters, or maybe because Aunt
Brocha is a very good-looking woman and Uncle
Leivik likes to show her how much he loves her.

When Aunt Brocha and Mother get involved in an
absorbing conversation, I steal away into my aunt's
bedroom. I examine a number of articles that are used
by women to make themselves better looking, such

as brushes, combs and various powders. My favourite
is a box of powder with a very soft powder puff inside
it. I open it up and put the powder puff on my face.
I close my eyes as I do it, and I can feel how my face
changes into a rare beauty as I bow to a huge audience
after a most difficult performance.

I wake up from that daydream when I hear my
mother calling me: 'Where are you, Hannah? It's time
to go home.'

I rush out of the fairy-tale bedroom with the linger-
ing smell of *Lebiaji Puch* following me.

Returning to our own house after such visits is
always hard for me. After my memorable trip to
Aunt Tzippah it leaves me bewildered. How is it all
arranged? Who decides what house each family should
have? Who measures and installs all the things, the
furniture, in each? And how come one house has a
lot of extraordinary things in it and another has none?

Forest in the Winter

On Sunday Vera's father, Leskov, stopped by to ask if we wanted to join him and another neighbour in gathering wood for the stove. They had hired a sledge and horse for the occasion.

Mamma was too weak to go. I offered to go for her. 'It should be nice to see the forest in the winter, if you'll take me along,' I added.

'Sure, come! We'll help,' he said.

'What a good neighbour you are, Mr Leskov.' Mamma sounded glad. 'I daren't do a lot of bending so soon after the operation.'

She piled loads of clothes on me. I could hardly move. 'Better not to be able to move than to be freezing,' she insisted. She gave me a piece of black bread in case I got hungry.

'What about the others?' I asked.

'They've probably got their own food.'

'Don't forget your gloves,' Raya reminded me. 'You'll freeze your fingers off, picking the wood up with your bare hands.'

We found somebody's gloves, twice as big as my hands. I got impatient. 'They're waiting,' I screamed.

Finally we were off to pick up Mr Leskov's friend. Sitting on the big sledge felt good, even though I didn't face the horse. He had little bells around his head and neck, and they jingled sweetly as we rode. We picked up Leskov's friend and gathered speed as we left the city. The cold made me sleepy.

We passed a small forest. The trees were covered with a white blanket of snow. They looked asleep, gathering strength for the spring. All the animals that inhabit the forest were resting under the cosy blanket of snow. The forest was quiet. Occasionally a branch welcomed the wind that helped brush off some of the snow to the ground. I watched a squirrel looking for a winter home, or maybe for some food. It listened to the bells and decided to hide from the strangers. We kept on riding, looking for a large area of dead wood. I felt cold, especially in my feet, which were not well protected.

Mr Leskov exclaimed, 'Here we are; this seems to be a good place to stop and start chopping wood.'

He took out an axe and a saw. His friend and he went to work, obviously glad to use their muscles and keep their bodies from freezing. I was given instructions to pick up the wood after it was chopped and make three neat little piles of it in the middle of the sledge.

The noise of the axe and the saw woke up the inhabitants of the forest. We could hear and see the shadows of the forest population moving about. I didn't like to disturb the small ones in their own habitat, and hoped that what they heard and reacted to was just a temporary diversion in their peaceful waiting time. I wanted to yell out to them: 'We will not hurt you. All we want is some wood for our stoves.' But I knew they used a different language and my yelling would only cause an argument between us. Meanwhile, I was standing and waiting to pick up more chopped wood so that I could take it to the sledge. But I didn't seem able to feel my feet, even though I was standing on them. I tried to move my toes. They didn't obey orders. I tried to lift one foot, then the other; all of this with great difficulty.

The cold air made my nose run. I wiped it with the big glove. It was beginning to snow. All the noises in

the forest stopped and the trees looked as if they were
dressed for a wedding.

Mr Leskov enjoyed chopping. The wood yielded
easily to his strong hands and fell to the ground on the
snow rug. His friend wasn't as familiar with the work-
ings of the axe and had given up after a few attempts.
He was now comfortably asleep, rocked by the silent
lullaby of the falling snow.

Carrying the wood to the sledge was getting more
difficult, since my feet refused to listen to me and the
snow stuck to my shoes. I felt as if each foot weighed
ten pounds.

Finally Mr Leskov announced, 'That's enough, or else
we'll become icicles and remain in the forest.'

We rode back. The horse could hardly see where he
was going. Snow was hanging on to his eyelashes, and
the warm steam from his breath formed a fog in front
of him. All the trees looked dressed up for a parade.
Everything was white, cold and unreal. I wanted to sleep
but instead I rubbed my feet, trying to bring them back
to life.

The road back seemed longer. Everyone was quiet.

Mr Leskov made small conversation with the horse.
'Get up there, I know how you feel. We are all cold
and hungry. Hurry up, there, come along.'

I saw no reaction from the poor horse. If anything,
he was slowing down as the going was getting harder.

We were almost home. It stopped snowing. The
streets were dark and slippery. Mr Leskov stopped as
close to the fence of the house as he could. Mamma
heard us arriving. She and my sister ran out to help us
bring the wood in. I could hardly walk. I was hoping
that Mother wouldn't notice anything, but she did.

'What's wrong with your feet?' she asked.

'Just cold and tired,' I said, not wanting to worry her.

We thanked Mr Leskov for his help and for the chopped wood. I was especially thankful to Mr Leskov for

letting me see the forest in the winter. I couldn't wait to tell Mamma how different it looked under the protection of the snow.

Mamma looked worried about my feet. She helped me to peel off the layers of clothing. The shoes and stockings came off last. My feet looked white, as if all the blood had left them. Mother brought in a pail of hot water. I put my feet in and still didn't feel a thing.

Mamma watched it all and pronounced: 'Hannah, your toes are frozen. Every time your feet are exposed to cold weather, you will have frozen toes.'

I didn't feel any pain. Secretly, I was beginning to feel special. Maybe now I'll be treated differently, even by my sister.

That night the small sacrifice of frozen feet, for Mother's comfort in having enough wood for the stove, made me feel good.

I Try to Look Like the Farmer's Wife

It was on a cool morning in May that Mamma and I got up early and she asked me to get some milk from the farm near the river. I had two hours before school and I liked the walk to the farm. The river, Sudost, surrounded now by wild, budding flowers, looked clear and quiet. The farmer's beautiful wife, all dressed up, was distributing the milk.

The story has it that she met her husband while swimming in the river, fell in love with him and with the land around the Sudost. They married, bought the land and half a dozen cows. Now they feed most of the population of Pochep, supplying them with milk and dairy products.

As I stood in line and stared at the farmer's wife, I noticed that her face looked as if it was painted by someone. Around her eyes there were two black lines, one on top of the eyes and the other under the eyes, which made the eyes look larger. Her cheeks were covered with a thick white paste and her lips were very red, as if they were bleeding. Yet the general effect was striking. Tied around her neck, she wore a black velvet ribbon. Her black hair was covered with a shiny oil. She looked like a picture and when she smiled I wanted to look at her for ever.

When I got close to the table where the farmer's wife was pouring the milk into the customers' containers, I quickly changed to the end of the line again and studied the eyes of the farmer's wife. I noticed that the black lines surrounding her eyes were made by hand. But what did she use? That remained a mystery to me.

I tried to think of a way to get black lines on my eyes and look like the farmer's wife, although I didn't have her beautiful face and was only twelve years old. When I returned home, I got an ingenious idea. Standing close to the oven, making sure Mother didn't see me, I took a few pieces of black coal from it, rubbed the coal on the brim of a pot in which a plant, a ficus, was growing in the dining-room. I touched it with my finger and put it on the lids of my eyes. I looked at myself in the mirror. All I needed now was the black velvet ribbon around my neck to look like the farmer's wife.

I went to school with my eyes as black as I could make them. I noticed that people looked at me. Did I see envy in their eyes or were they frightened by me? Secretly, I was proud of my invention and felt closer than ever to make-believe.

Questions about my health came from teachers as well as from some of the girls in my class. My sister, Raya, was ashamed to be seen with me. She whispered something when no one was looking, but I pretended not to hear her. Sonia Greenberg came over to me between classes and asked, 'Is something wrong with you, Hannah?' She smiled, but tried to look concerned.

It took about two weeks of interest, pity and shock. After that, everyone seemed to have made peace with the fact that something was wrong with my eyes. Everyone thought it, but not Mamma. She kept looking and asking questions, hoping to get an honest answer.

'Tell me the truth, Hannah. What's wrong with your eyes? Do they hurt you? Did someone suggest a new soap?'

To all the questions my answer never changed: 'I am

fine, Mamma. My eyes are fine. They are just black now.'

And so I lived with my make-believe eyes until . . . until one day, Mamma announced: 'Hannah, I have made an appointment with an eye doctor. We want to make sure that there is nothing wrong with your eyes.'

'Mamma, don't we need some milk? Let me go to the farm and get some,' I said. I had to compare my art work with the eyes of the farmer's wife before my secret was discovered. If I only had a black velvet ribbon to complete the picture of my make-believe.

It felt good to see the serene farm again where nothing seemed to interfere with nature's schedule – the daisies with their yellow centres and white petals, the lilies and the forget-me-nots – all of them opening up because it was their time to do so. The cows were cheerfully chewing the young grass before it came to full growth. The other animals waited cheerfully for their mealtime and the population of Pochep waited patiently in line to get fresh milk. The smell of the pine trees sweetened the air of spring.

I looked at the table from which the containers of milk were filled. The farmer's wife, with the black ribbon and black eyes, wasn't there.

I asked the woman who was next to me: 'Where is the farmer's wife?'

'She had to leave the farm,' came the response. 'Something urgent came up.'

I felt disappointed and lost. How could I compare myself with the model whose example I had tried to follow?

Tomorrow I'll have to wash the black off my eyes, I thought, otherwise, Mamma will take me to the doctor and my whole scheme will be discovered.

I got the milk and bade a sad goodbye to the farm, the river and all the creatures who so willingly obey the laws of nature.

A Piano of Our Own?

On Tuesday at two o'clock in the afternoon I went for my piano lesson as usual. I played a piece by Bach. Madame Smirnova listened. After I had finished, she got up, picked up a piece of paper from the table and came back to me, saying, 'I have here an address where a very old piano is for sale. Do you think, Hannah, your mother could afford to buy it? You wouldn't have to go to Mrs Greenberg to practise anymore.'

I took my hands off the keyboard and asked, 'Madame Smirnova, how much do they want for the piano?' Afraid to hear the answer, I listened attentively.

'The people who are selling it, the Vasilievs, want twenty-five roubles. It's long and very narrow. You would first have to measure it to see if you have enough space for it.'

The thought of having our own piano made me suddenly very hot. 'Let me take the address and I'll speak to Mother,' I said hesitantly, knowing what Mamma's answer would be. I wrote down the name and address on the first page of my music book and continued with my lesson. What am I ready to give up for the privilege of having a piano? Even the possibility of such a thing made me dizzy.

I got home and tried to look as if nothing unusual had happened. First, I had to find the best time to tell

Mamma. Then I must have a plan whereby the twenty-five roubles for the piano could be saved by cutting some other expenses. Which ones?

I could not wait too long. The idea of having our own piano was too important to keep to myself. The following day I began by saying to Mamma, 'Wouldn't it be wonderful if we had a piano of our own?'

Mamma laughed as she answered, 'Are you dreaming, Hannah? Why not begin with a cow of our own? Then all of us could eat butter, drink milk. With a piano, only you could play it just a little. And where would you put a piano?'

I surprised myself by saying, 'Mamma, there is a piano for sale, really cheap.' I rushed my words, afraid to stop. 'It's long and narrow, very old, but most keys still play. If we are interested, Madame Smirnova said we should measure it first to see how much room it would need.' I stopped talking. I could feel the silence in the room. Mamma didn't answer. She moved to look out of the eating-room window. Her back was facing me so I could not see what she was thinking.

My mouth was dry. I was losing courage. What do I say now? I heard Madame Smirnova saying to me, 'Don't give up, Hannah.'

Oh, yes. Talk about money. 'Mamma, would you like to know how much they are asking for the piano?' I tried to be funny. 'Do you want to guess?' There was no answer. I had to go on before Mamma left the room. 'I don't need a new dress every Passover. I am growing faster now and probably could wear Raya's clothes. If I don't have a new dress for the next five years, how much money would we save?'

From a voice near the window came a rushed reply, 'Hannah, you cannot save money you don't have.'

Miracle of miracles, I had a new idea: 'I'll go to all my aunts and uncles and ask them for a loan. The piano will cost only twenty-five roubles. I have three uncles and two aunts on your side,' I went on hopefully, 'and three uncles and one aunt on Father's side. If each of them would lend us two roubles, we'd have enough even for getting it over to our house.'

'Drop that plan, Hannah,' Mother said. I suppose she was too proud to let anyone know we had no money.

Mamma spoke again, slowly. 'I don't mind asking my brother, Leib. He is the youngest. If he has the money, he'll lend it to me and I can pay it back within a year, slowly. We'll go tomorrow to measure the piano and if it isn't too big for our rooms, I'll speak to Uncle Leib.'

I jumped for joy. I wanted to run to Mamma and hug her and kiss her and thank her, but I knew she wouldn't like it. So all I said was, 'Oh, Mamma, thank you, thank you. I'll learn to play really well.'

But why did she agree so quickly and readily? Maybe she could tell by my breathlessness and sweating face how much I wanted the piano.

Mamma asked to see the address. 'It's not too far from us, but quite close to Belaia Street where your piano teacher lives. We'll go tomorrow and tell the Vasilievs that we are interested in buying the piano if we have enough room for it.'

It was Friday morning. We got ready to go to the Vasilievs'. Mamma told me not to put the good dress on. I asked why not and she explained, 'They'll think we are richer than we are and might ask more for the piano.'

Was Mamma wrong? I didn't dare to argue with her. The walk seemed long and tedious. The Vasilievs were glad to see us, after Mamma told them why we had come. The house looked small and bare. The piano occupied most of it. Mr Vasiliev gave us the reason for selling the piano – their daughter, who played, had moved to another city. Mother let them know that we had to measure the piano before we could buy it.

I looked at the piano. The wood was light brown.

Some of it was cracked, due to age, I guessed. The keyboard was covered by the lid. I was afraid to touch it. We'd have to get used to each other slowly. Mother took the measurements. The piano was long and narrow. Mamma promised to come back on Monday after she had measured our room where the piano was to be installed.

The Vasilievs had a friend who had a wagon long enough to put the piano on and bring it to us.

The next step was a trip to Uncle Leib. Mother wanted to go there alone.

I had three long days of waiting before I could hope to see the piano in our house. Three long days of doubt: will our room be big enough to hold a piano? Will Uncle Leib be kind enough to lend the money?

While I was waiting for Mother to return from Uncle Leib's, I read a history book about Peter the Great. He also wanted many new things for his Russia. Some of his wishes came true, just as I hoped that Mamma would come with twenty-five roubles for the piano. That would make my wish come true.

Mamma came back. I heard her. I ran to meet her and asked, 'Did you get the money, Mamma? Was Uncle nice to you?' I kept asking so many questions that Mother didn't have a chance to answer. Finally, I stopped talking and got a calm answer.

'Yes, thank God for my brother Leib. He does help when I am in need.'

'When will you go to the Vasilievs to ask them to send the piano over?' I asked. I knew I sounded impatient. 'Is our room big enough, Mamma?'

'Yes, the room is big enough if we aren't in it.' I hoped Mamma was joking. I closed my eyes and dreamt away about me and the piano.

It was Monday morning. I had to go to school. Mamma was going to see about the piano without me. She didn't want me to miss school. It was hard for me to pay attention to the classes. All I thought about was the long, narrow piano with the cracked wood on top. I couldn't wait to get home. I ran all the way. I saw the wagon coming back from our street. I opened the *kalitka*, ran into the house and saw the piano. Slowly, I came near it, opened the lid, played a minor scale and swallowed the tears of welcome for a wish come true.

I Am Still a Child – How Long?

I felt longer, I mean taller, but not wider.

'Mamma, am I taller this year than I was last year?'

'Of course you are. Every year you are growing a little taller.'

Mamma seemed annoyed with my question. She didn't share my concern. One day I would wake up and feel like a woman. I'd have hips and breasts like other girls my age, which I don't show now.

Maybe these feminine charms are distributed unevenly. Some have, and some haven't. Like money. Who is in charge? Mother didn't like to talk about it. She thought I was too young to know. My sister Raya knew, but wouldn't share her knowledge with me.

Walking home from school, I got behind some older girls who were going my way, and tried to listen to their conversation. They were speaking about a period, but they didn't mention commas or writing, so I knew it had nothing to do with grammar. I slowed down and listened carefully.

This is what I heard them say: 'My Mamma warned me not to run too much, and in general to be careful when I have my period.'

Her friend looked at her with admiration as she said: 'You are lucky. Isn't this the second month that you have had it? I haven't even started and I am as old as you are – only two months' difference between our birthdays.'

Trying not to miss a word, I walked so close to them that I almost fell on top of them. But at the end, I still hardly knew what they were talking about. My curiosity was aroused and I decided right then and there to ask Mamma about it.

The following day was Friday, a busy day for Mother, because she had to cook enough on that day for two days. Saturday, the Sabbath, was a day of rest. Jewish people were not supposed to ride, cook or clean on that day. But they were allowed to talk. I couldn't wait until tomorrow so I started to follow Mamma around, from the big stove in the small hall to the eating-room, offering to help with the preparation of the two meals. I was given the job of peeling a whole bag of potatoes, probably the mainstay of our dinner for the two days.

I began cautiously: 'Mamma, in a few months I'll be thirteen years old. Does anything special happen to a girl when she is thirteen? Should I know what to expect? Is a mother to tell a girl? Is it something I ought to be ashamed of?' I looked at Mother.

She had that surprised expression, as if she wanted to say, 'Here we go . . .' But she was silent.

I got up, stopped peeling potatoes and, with a breaking voice, shouted: 'Mamma, please, you never tell me anything. Tell me, when will I begin to get my menstrual period like other girls do? When?'

The surprise on Mother's face changed to shock. She cried out: 'Oh, my God, what kind of talk is that? Who told you to ask all these questions? Nature takes its course. When it comes you'll know it. You're no different from others . . . I didn't know about it until it came. Why should you? '

I also raised my voice, 'It's different now,' I defended myself. 'The girls talk about it. I am probably the only one who doesn't know what to expect.'

Mamma heard tears in my voice. She came over to me, put her hands on my shoulders, gave me a little squeeze, and tried to reassure me by saying, 'I'll tell you what I can. Sit down.'

I sat down. Mamma wiped her hands on the apron she was wearing and sat down next to me. She began by telling me, 'The town we lived in when I was your age was even smaller than Pochep. When I was twelve and a half my mother died. Father was in the Russian army. An aunt we had never seen before came to stay with us and to take care of my three brothers and two sisters. I was the youngest.

'There was no school in that town. The boys went to a Jewish school. The girls learned a little from the boys. A young Russian woman would come to do some heavy work and help in the small store that kept the family alive. The woman's name was Aliona.

'One day Aliona called on me when I was just getting out of bed. "Frayde," she said, "is something hurting you?"

'To which I answered, "No, nothing hurts me. Why do you ask?"

'Aliona crossed herself and murmured, "Lord, be merciful. Frayda has now entered womanhood".'

Mamma raised her voice as she continued, 'Aliona,' I said, 'stop talking in riddles. What do you see?'

' "I see blood on your bed. That is your first menstrual period, which you'll be getting every month now and which makes you a woman. Here are rags. May the Lord be with you," and she crossed herself again.'

Mamma got up and continued, 'I cannot tell you any more than I know myself.' She picked up the peeled potatoes and told me that when she saw blood on my bed, she'd know I was a woman.

I remained seated and was glad not to be a woman yet.

I remember the following Saturday as a special day.

Mother didn't have to work very hard, as the dinner had been cooked on Friday. After dinner, which consisted as usual of meat and potatoes (a combination that keeps its taste even after standing in the oven for twenty-four hours), Mamma took Raya and me to the square for the first time, the only place where young people took walks on Fridays, Saturdays and Sundays.

The square was only five or six city blocks long. Situated in the middle of the city, it separated the rich houses from the poor neighbourhoods. In the early spring it was particularly appealing, since it was surrounded by young birch trees with small flowers around them in bright colours of red, yellow and blue.

The young people who walked back and forth in the square were both men and women. Some of them were teenagers: girls, who could not wait to be eyed by boys; the boys were there to look and choose. Sometimes a small group of two or three would stop and the boys would introduce themselves to the girls. Excitement could be seen and heard by the squealing and laughing of both males and females. The fact that Mamma had offered to take us to the square made it a memorable event. It must have been compensation for the skimpy information on the period.

Dear Diary,

It's time to share my thoughts with you. Some of the events, the echoes of which are slowly coming even to our small town, aren't a secret anymore. When thoughts become words written down by someone, they are there for ever, waiting to be read. The year is 1914. We learn in school that war between Germany and Russia has been raging for some time. Russia orders general mobilisation. Neither Papa nor his brothers are involved; but I still don't know about Grandpa, who is in the reserves. The word 'war' has a terrible sound to it. We learn from history that most of the land, not only of Russia, but also of other countries, is annexed or appropriated by victories in wars. And the war is essentially a fight for recognition of every nationality. What we don't learn in school is why men have to die for it. The war is spreading, with every nation, or almost every nation, participating in it.

Mamma is telling us that food is getting more expensive and harder to get. But, dear Diary, I have other troubles, too. I am hardly growing. Maybe I don't eat enough. Once a week I measure my chest with a tape measure, just about an eighth of an inch bigger, hardly visible to the naked eye. Now, that's a secret. Even Mamma doesn't know that I measure myself so often. No hips, no breasts, no period. I should have been born a boy. No boy will look at me. Is this for ever? Will it change? When? So far I don't even like healthy teenage boys. I like them a little bit on the sick side. If a young man looks pale he has a good chance with me. I know it's peculiar, but so is war, and men who are maimed, wounded and dead. That is also strange.

Dear Diary, what I hear at home is even stranger: friends of my parents and some of our relatives all pray for Germany – not Russia, but Germany – to win the war. I asked Uncle Mendel, my mother's brother, who is called 'the educated one' because he is always reading a dictionary, to tell me why they want Germany to win. His answer: they consider Germany a country of culture that will therefore treat the Jewish people with less prejudice. Others want Russia to be punished by God for its intolerance and inhumanity to them. Well, DD, this is what he said to me: 'War is the cruellest way to settle anything.' Maybe I still must learn a lot before I have answers to many things in life. Now, I want the war to stop before anyone wins. Is that strange?

Genia

One of my greatest childhood fears was the outhouse toilet. The family moved twice during those years and still the toilet remained in the courtyard, open to anyone who needed it.

Especially frightening was to enter the toilet at night and search for the open hole. Most of all I feared the invisible creatures I imagined existed there. It began to interfere with my bodily functions.

Mother found a way to ease my fears by giving me a lighted candle when I needed to use the toilet at night.

One day on my way to the toilet I met Genia, who was returning from it. Genia was a beautiful young girl. Tall and slender, she had large black eyes and shiny black hair tied with a ribbon. Soft spoken, yet full of laughter, Genia seemed to enjoy speaking to me whenever we met. That pleased me very much since Genia was fourteen and a half years old, and I only twelve and a half.

Genia's family lived in the front of the courtyard. They had a small sweet shop. An older sister and Genia helped their mother in the store while their father, being religious, spent most of the time in the synagogue. Whenever we met, Genia would talk mostly about her family.

Once I asked, 'What school do you go to, Genia?'

'I go to the high school on Kusnechnaia. It's a long walk to get there. What about you, Hannah?' she asked.

Should I keep it a secret that because of the Jewish quota I had been put in a class two grades below my age? After a short hesitation I decided against it and told her the truth. Genia wasn't surprised.

The next time we met we talked about our favourite subjects in school. I was glad that both of us liked maths. I told Genia how much I loved to return to school every autumn ... all the new things I expected to discover ... the change from home to school served as a window to the world. She wasn't surprised to hear this from me because she felt the same way. I kept my love of music a secret from her, remembering the negative reaction of my family to it.

Once, when we met at the usual place, Genia invited me to visit her at home and meet the family. We made an appointment for the following Monday after school.

On Monday I told Mother about the invitation, describing Genia in glowing terms. I omitted the fact that she was two and a half years older. Whenever Mother and I held serious talks, she would always say, in answer to my questions, 'You are too young to know,' or, 'Wait, you'll know it soon enough, when you are older.' I thought it best to keep one little secret from Mamma.

In preparation for the visit, I scrubbed my face and hands, combed my hair, removed some spots from my dress and appeared at the appointed time in front of Genia's apartment. As I entered, I was glad to see that it was furnished just as sparsely and was as grey-looking as our own. That freed me of some of my shyness.

I met Genia's mother and sister, after which both of them left for the store. Genia and I remained alone and could talk. Genia showed me her guitar, and impulsively I burst out: 'I'm taking piano lessons.' I looked at Genia to see what impression my special secret made on her.

'Are you really learning how to play? I like to play the guitar, but no lessons. I sing as I play, mostly sad songs. I'll play for you some time.'

'You will, really?' I was excited at the prospect but too shy to offer to play the piano for her. Having heard the advanced students of Madame Smirnova, I thought my playing wouldn't sound good enough. So it was much to my own surprise that I heard myself saying, 'I'm learning a new piece, a galliard by Bach. Would you like to hear it one day?'

'Oh, yes. What is a galliard?' enquired Genia.

'A galliard is a cheerful piece of music originally written for a social dance in the seventeenth century. It was danced by the peasants and later adapted by the French aristocracy.'

'You know so much,' said Genia, obviously impressed by all the information.

'Our piano teacher tells us a little bit of the history of each piece we play.'

'Aren't you lucky?' envied Genia.

'Yes, I'm also lucky to have you as a friend,' I said, blushing. 'It must be getting late. I should be going home.' My shyness returned as I was saying goodbye to Genia.

I ran home. Mother was there. I burst out, 'Mamma, I love my new friend. She's beautiful, she's smart, and she plays the guitar.' I hugged Mother and began to dance with her, repeating, 'I have . . . a friend, and I love her . . . I have a good friend . . .'

Mother didn't share her daughter's enthusiasm. She yelled, 'Hannah, stop it, stop it. You're getting me dizzy. Just tell me, how did you like their apartment and what did you talk about?'

But I was hurt by Mother's indifference and said, 'I'll tell you later.'

As time went on, Genia and I saw each other often.

After each meeting I would tell Mother about it with great excitement.

'You know, Mamma, Genia and I are such good friends. We like the same things. She is sad sometimes, and so am I, but neither of us knows why.'

As promised, Genia did play the guitar and sang what she called her 'sad songs' for me. When she sang, her eyes would get darker and deeper. I felt like crying when I heard Genia play and sing.

I practised diligently to learn the galliard and played it for Genia. It was the first time that Genia had seen and heard anyone play the piano. Sharing a love for music made our friendship lasting and important to me.

Then suddenly, just before the summer vacation from school, I didn't see Genia for a whole week. I looked for her through the windows of her apartment, I tried to catch her when she might be going to the outhouse, but Genia seemed to have disappeared. I missed her and on Friday afternoon stopped at the store and asked her sister if Genia was at home and if I could see her.

Genia's sister, Nina, looked tired and not friendly. She said, 'Genia has a bad cold. It's best for both of you, Hannah, if you wait to see her when she gets better.'

'Will you please tell her I stopped by, and hope she gets better soon?'

But Genia wasn't getting better. The cold turned into 'a nasty cough that won't go away,' as Nina said.

I stopped at the store every other day to find out how Genia was doing. I didn't understand why I couldn't see my friend, and spent a lot of time watching the store or the door to Genia's apartment, anxious to find out anything about Genia's health.

One time I saw an older man entering the store. He carried a small black case. I guessed that it might be the doctor, knowing what a doctor's case looked like from the occasions when Father needed a doctor.

After the man with the black case had left, I went down to the courtyard and quietly entered the store. Genia's mother was there alone. She was crying. When she saw me, she wiped her tears and tried to smile as she said hello.

'How is Genia? What did the doctor say?' I asked.

It took some time before Genia's mother could answer. In a whisper, she said: 'Genia has consumption. The doctor called it tuberculosis.'

I didn't know what kind of illness it was. Mumbling a quick 'thank you', I ran out of the store.

When I got home, I asked Mother, but she also didn't know. My sister Raya knew. She explained, 'It's a very dangerous illness of the lungs.'

I ran downstairs and stopped in front of the door to Genia's apartment. I didn't dare to go in.

Two days later I saw several men in front of the store. They were talking to each other. A little further away, on the road, stood a horse-driven wagon. Running from one man to another I asked each one the same question, 'How is my friend? How is Genia?'

Several of them either didn't understand or ignored me. At last, one of them said, 'Genia died. Was she a friend of yours?' I didn't answer.

At home, I kept asking everyone, 'Is it possible for Genia to die? Isn't she too young to die?'

At dinner time Mother urged me to eat something, but I wasn't hungry. I went to bed, and before crying myself to sleep kept on whispering, 'I miss you, Genia, please, come back, come back.'

Next morning I felt an anger swallowing me up, anger at everyone who had taken Genia away from me. I refused to eat, refused to talk to anyone. I disappeared for hours, going to places I had been to with Genia, taking the same walks I had taken with her, played the galliard several times just because I had played it for Genia.

On the third day Mother, fearing for my health, tried to persuade me to eat by telling me, 'Your friend Genia would want you to eat. I know she would.'

'I cannot eat, Mamma,' I forced myself to say, after I looked at my mother's worried face.

'Drink some milk, then,' offered Mother, as a compromise.

I took the glass of milk to my lips and swallowed some. The cool milk felt good to my parched throat.

Hannah Discovers Bach

Our old piano, with three soundless keys, was gradually becoming an important member of my family. I shared my joys and sorrows with it. I paid dearly for that privilege: no new dresses for many Passovers to come. How many? It was up to Mother to decide.

Now that I didn't have to practise the lessons on Mrs Greenberg's piano, music became a more exciting part of my life. I tried to share it with the family but my sister Raya made fun of it and Mother tolerated it as something temporary. So I learned to keep my love of music a secret, sharing it with the teacher who had introduced me to it, with the piano on which I played, and with my diary, where I could speak of it. Every new composer whose music I learned became my friend. The newest discovery was Johann Sebastian Bach. When I played his simplified pieces for beginners I loved them for their variety.

Madame Smirnova liked to talk a little about each piece I played. She would start like this: 'Today, Hannah, I want to tell you about a composer who wrote a lot of church music as well as music for dances, popular at his time with the upper classes. He starts with a saraband or a pavan, which are slow, sombre dances, and ends with dances like the courante, minuet, gavotte, all of them written in lively tempos. Of course, you are playing them in the simplified form.'

Madame Smirnova played as she talked. Though I didn't know what to listen to first, her playing or her words, I loved these sessions. Her tales would carry me to beautiful rooms, far away, where men and women would dress in the brilliant colours of the day and would glide languidly to the music of Johann Sebastian Bach. His music was as varied as it was prolific.

Before long, Madame Smirnova would have me learning the two- and three-part 'inventions', and playing Bach would become a daily menu. I wrote in my diary:

Dear Diary,
I haven't told you the secrets of my life for some time. On the surface, nothing has changed. I feel just as small and undeveloped as I was last year. What I want to share with you are the important changes of my heart. We have a new teacher of maths in the gymnazia. I think she likes me. I simply adore her, as well as what she teaches. She has a small face and large brown eyes. Her olive skin is soft and her black hair smooth. Her smile is warm. And maths is a logical science. All you have to do is think a little. Sometimes she asks me to explain the theorems to other students. Can you imagine that? Do I do it? Of course I do, and get a five plus – the best grade. Is that why I love her? No, no, no. How can you even think it? I love her because she is intelligent – you have to be, to teach maths. She is also kind. Mathematics is fun to learn, and to have a teacher who likes me is my good fortune. At the same time, DD, I have a new composer friend: Johann Sebastian Bach. Even his name sounds like music. And Vera Ivanovna, the maths teacher, has something in common with J S Bach. That's my secret. I can tell it only to you. After I figure out an algebra problem and play a two-part invention on my old piano, I feel peaceful, even though there is a war in the world.

Why should governments want to kill people just to gain a new piece of land? You and I cannot answer that question. But why can't I share my love of music and maths with my family? Maybe you can answer that. There are too many unanswered questions. Well, DD, I'd better say goodbye for now. I think I'll go to Madame Smirnova's studio to listen to some advanced students playing on a good piano. That's another secret of mine. I go there and listen for as long as I can to students playing. DD, I am glad to have had this chance to talk to you.

I ran out secretly, as I always did, and ten minutes later I knocked at Madame Smirnova's studio. Her maid opened the door.

She greeted me and said, 'Today you are lucky. There is an all-Bach programme which the advanced students will play for each other.'

I got myself arranged on a small bench in the waiting room, ready to receive the pleasure of hearing good music. I couldn't tell where Bach's music would send me this time. Place and time were forgotten. When the music stopped, I became aware that it was evening and the streets were dark. Without saying goodbye to anyone, I left the studio and ran all the way home.

Opening the *kalitka* to the courtyard, I heard familiar voices. Mother and Raya were talking agitatedly. I stood still and listened.

'Did you look for her?' asked Mamma.

'Of course I did. I couldn't find her,' answered Raya.

'You should have watched over her, Raya, she is still a child.' Mother sounded worried.

'I must tell you, Mother,' Raya's voice grew hoarse, 'my sister and I live under the same roof, but since our visit to Aunt Chaya-Esther, when she lied to me about Father's arrival, I can't tell what she is thinking; and when she talks to me, all I can do is laugh.'

'Give her a chance, Raya, she needs to grow up.'

'She is certainly slow about it.'

I felt a lump in my throat. Swallowing hard I walked into the house. I entered the living-room and faced Mother and my sister.

'Sorry to be late,' I said. Mother looked relieved.

'Where have you been, Hannah? We looked all over for you.'

'I was listening to Bach.' Reluctantly, I had to reveal my secret. Mother insisted on knowing more.

'The name is unfamiliar. Do we know him?' she asked.

'Mother, Bach is a composer,' I said, instructing her patiently.

'I don't care what his profession is, if we don't know him, you shouldn't have gone to see him. You missed dinner. Have something to eat.'

I felt that Mamma's tone was softer. I continued with the educational approach. 'Mamma, Bach is a composer of music. He lived a long time ago. His music lives on.'

'If it's music, why did you have to go anywhere? You have a piano of your own to play on now.'

'I wanted to hear the advanced students of Madame Smirnova. I went to her studio.'

I was beginning to sound tired. 'I will not eat anything. I am not hungry.'

I wanted to stop talking. I went to bed and the music of Bach was still ringing in my ears.

Am I a Woman Now?

My ears were open but not my eyes. I heard my mother singing. It was 'sad song' day. I knew that song well. Mother had told me all about it. The words of that song were by Necrasov, who lived in the nineteenth century. Mamma said he was popular because his poems were sad. The poem of this song was about a man just released from prison. He walks out on a big road. He is free, but he has nowhere to go. He likes the warm sunshine that smiles at him, yet he is sad and lonely.

I opened my eyes. I felt something strange happening to my body. I remembered: in another month I'll be thirteen. I counted on my fingers – thirty, thirty-one, two, three, four, five, six, seven, eight, nine, ten, eleven, twelve. In forty more days I'll be thirteen – a woman. I looked at my bed and saw little red spots near my body.

I jumped out of bed and ran to my mother crying, 'Mamma, Mamma, I think I just became a woman. What do I do? Tell me, you've got to tell me.'

My mother laughed at the innocent remarks of her daughter. She said, 'Yes, my dear, you are a woman now, but only for three or four days, after which you become a little girl again.'

I was not pleased with my mother's answer. I wanted to tell the whole world, especially the girls in school, that now I was one of them. They talked so proudly

about having their period. But, it was summer . . . no
school, and most of my friends were away. I wanted to
know more.

'Why do I have to wait, Mamma, until I marry to
feel like a woman? Tell me, why?'

I heard Mother laugh, but didn't see her. Her back
was turned. She tore a clean old sheet into small pieces.
She wrapped one piece around my waist, and others
were put between my legs and pinned to the one around
my waist.

I was fascinated by this procedure and was beginning
to feel important. My mind was full of questions.

'Will I like boys less now, and young men more,
Mamma?'

I got no answer. Too excited to give up, I continued,
'Tell me, Mother, is it true that if I let a young man kiss
me, I might get pregnant? Tell me, *something*, please.'

'Hannah, you are too excited. Just be happy that you
are having your period like all girls your age. You are
too young to worry about men.'

'Mamma, don't they tell you in a synagogue what to
say to your daughter when she becomes a woman?'

'I have to go to the store,' Mother said as she put her
jacket on. 'We'll talk more later.'

I began to feel unwell and weak. I laid down and fell
asleep. I didn't sleep long and woke up with a groan.
Questions were still dancing around in my mind. But
there was no one to talk to. I grabbed my little diary
and wrote:

Dear Diary,
Here I am, weak, sleepy and not well. I am losing
my good blood. But I am a woman for only four days
while the blood separates from my body. After that
I turn back into the little girl that I am. That's what
my mother says. Can you help me, DD, to figure it
out? I fell asleep for half an hour and I want to tell

you what I dreamt about. A special message came from God. I knew it was from Him because it flew in from the sky so it had to be from God. It fell into my hands. I opened it. The message read: 'To whom it may concern: Anyone who expects to become a woman, beware. Losing blood is not the only way to it. Obedience, patience, also womanly attributes, such as breasts, hips, breasts, hips, breasts, hips . . .' I couldn't read it any further so I woke up with a groan. DD, why didn't Mamma tell me that? She probably didn't want me to know about it.

And the war rages on. I hear all the grown-up people talking about it. Men are dying. Maybe there won't be any men left after the war ends, if it will ever end. I see a group of people on the square reading the bulletin with all the names of those 'who have given their lives for the Motherland in the World War of 1915'. I want somebody to talk to me. You, DD, can only listen and I am glad of that. I'd better stop talking to you, DD, I hear my sister Raya coming.

I looked at my sister as if seeing her for the first time.

'Hello, Hannah,' Raya said. 'You look as if you've never seen me before.'

'You look so much older since I saw you last, and it was only a day ago,' I said, surprised at the discovery.

'Maybe you didn't look long enough. You look older to me, too.'

'Today I became a woman,' I announced proudly, while working out our age difference. I would be thirteen in a month, so Raya would be seventeen. No wonder she looked older. She really looked like a woman, I thought, with envy.

Raya ran over to me, embraced me, and practically yelled, 'Congratulations, my dear sister.' She sounded relieved, as if now that I was also a woman our differences would disappear.

'Raya, Mamma told me that I was a woman only while I was having my period, and after the four days I will be a child again.'

Raya laughed. 'She was probably teasing you.'

I wanted a more definite answer.

The following morning I got up and the first thing I did was to check my entrance into womanhood. 'Yes, blood doesn't lie.' That's what Mamma had said once. It was flowing freely, reminding me of my new responsibilities.

After the usual breakfast of tea with bread and butter, I had what I thought was a good idea . . . to take a walk in the little square where I had seen, not long ago, girls and boys exchanging glances and giggles. I wanted to see what it was like now, but I would need Mother's permission or have someone with me. I sat down on my bed, put my head in my hands to think clearer.

I saw my sister Raya, passing by. I jumped up and ran after her, screaming, 'Raya, will you take me to the square? Mamma will let me go if I tell her that you'll walk with me.'

'When do you want to go?' asked Raya, with a sly smile, and suggested Friday as 'the best day for it'. 'I'll tell Mamma about our plan,' she added. I felt that Raya sounded sure of the plan's success, now that she was in charge.

However, I had at least a dozen unresolved problems: should I wear something new, to indicate a change in me? Should I have my hair up, now that I was a woman, or down, so as not to scare the boys away? I wondered: should I wear socks or silk stockings, as the grown-up girls did? . . . forgetting that I didn't even have any.

On Friday I didn't have to remind my sister of our appointment. She remembered. I took my time getting ready. I washed my hair and decided to wear it down. I scrubbed my hands, face and neck, and pulled the hair back and tied it with a blue ribbon. I wore the good dress, of course, and wondered why Raya remained in her skirt and blouse.

We started out early. Mamma gave us two Kopeks for two glasses of sparkling water in case we got thirsty. I was excited. How would a woman feel, being in my place? I didn't know, but I felt as if I were opening a new door to my life.

The square was almost empty. A cool breeze made the leaves of the birch trees fall. Raya and I walked around the square once without seeing anyone. Then, just as we completed the circle for the second time, a group of three boys entered the square. Two of them looked like giants to me. They were probably about sixteen or seventeen. A little behind them was a younger boy, walking slowly with a limp.

Suddenly I felt uneasy. The whole scheme lost its appeal to me. The two boys began to walk faster when they saw us. I looked at the younger boy behind them, limping along slowly. I wanted to talk to him but couldn't. My tongue froze in my mouth.

I was frightened and longed to return to the time when I had taken my first walk in the square, looking for a pale boy with a cough or a sore throat, in need of help. I grabbed my sister's arm and pulled at her sleeve, but Raya didn't respond.

I began to run ahead, crying, 'Let's go home, let's go home.'

Raya ran after me, yelling, 'Wait, Hannah, wait for me.'

The two boys were running after us, shouting, 'Hey, don't run away. All we want is to walk with you.'

Breathlessly, Raya and I opened the door to the safety of home . . . as the gathering clouds darkened the streets in the promise of rain.

The House We Lived In

The house we lived in was built in a courtyard along with two other houses. The entrance to it was through the kitchen. There might have been another entrance for guests, but we never used it. The rooms in the house were small, and divided by thin walls. The living-room, which I began to call the piano-room, had two large windows facing the street. The rest of the rooms were windowless.

From the kitchen, one entered into a room that housed a round table, two benches and four chairs. That was the room used for eating, mostly. Sometimes the floor there was also used for sleeping.

To the right of the eating-room, there were two small bedrooms. The bigger of the two was used by Mamma and Papa; the smaller one by me and my sister. We had no electricity. At night we used a kerosene lamp in the eating-room.

The darkness in the bedroom, as in the outhouse, made me fear the nights. Tears and nightmares were my frequent companions before and during sleep.

When I was very little, four or five years old, I had very often to remain in the house alone. Afraid to stay there, I would run out and sit on the doorstep. I loved to observe the comings and goings of the neighbours who lived in the other houses in the courtyard. I'd watch them for hours, looking at their faces and listening to them talk. When I got a little older, I began to tell Mother what they said and how they said it by imitating them. I noticed that it made Mother laugh every time I did it. I repeated the performance gladly whenever she'd asked me what the neighbours were talking about.

I would begin with my favourite imitation of a young woman who stuttered badly. She would close one eye as she was telling a story and stick her tongue out as she mispronounced every word. Spasmodically a shower of saliva would dance around her mouth as she spoke.

Unlike the many houses I had to pass on the way to school, whose gardens yards looked green at springtime and full of flowers in the summer, nothing grew in the courtyard of the house we lived in. It always looked barren, with the dusty ground turning to mud when it rained. One lonely birch tree did grow in the back of the courtyard. Each spring it would dress up with its green leaves around it, but because it was close to the outhouse I never stopped long enough to look at it.

Our street seemed empty most of the time, as if people had found better ways to get to wherever they were going. Bigger and better houses were built in streets that went upwards, like Mrs Greenberg's house, on whose piano I used to practise my lessons. One had practically to climb a mountain to get there, whereas our house was on a street going downhill. When it rained, we had to jump over big puddles and I always got my feet wet.

Once I had passed my thirteenth birthday, I was ashamed to have anyone see me sitting on the steps of the house, as if I had nothing to do. I could always share my loneliness now with the piano, and with my diary, where I wrote how disappointing being thirteen could be: yet I had been ready to skip being eleven and twelve to get to thirteen faster.

The months of my thirteenth year were passing with little change. My sister still considered me too young to be her equal. Mother's need for my help to clean and scrub continued, though she became more interested in knowing where I was going and how long I would be there.

The war continued its pace of death and destruction, with more nations joining. Rumour had it that the United States was planning to get in, too. Food was becoming scarce, and some of it unobtainable. Father was still out of town a lot, but stayed closer to home. Whenever he got back he'd bring us sugar and salt, which were difficult items to find in the stores.

Then a miraculous thing happened to the family Kagan. An order from the local government, posted everywhere, read: FAMILIES WITH NO LITTLE CHILDREN WHO HAVE MORE THAN ONE ROOM MUST TAKE IN ANOTHER FAMILY WHO HAS HAD TO EVACUATE FROM TOWNS CLOSE TO THE FRONT.

A city government official came to the house, introduced himself, and when invited to come in, looked at the rooms and spoke to Mother about the new ruling. I followed them around and listened to the official's every word. Something new, somebody new. My curiosity was aroused. The new family might even speak a different language – maybe French. I was just beginning to study French at school. The city official advised Mother to move personal belongings from at least two rooms to make sure that the new family would have a place to sleep.

When Mother asked him when they were arriving, the official answered, 'I don't have the exact time of their arrival as yet, but the next family that will need lodging immediately are three adults and a child. They are on top of the list of those who had to escape from their homes.'

Before leaving, the official mentioned a very important detail. He said, 'I shouldn't forget to tell you, Madame Kagan, that you will get paid according to the existing scale.'

I could tell that Mother tried to conceal a sigh of relief. We certainly could use the money. My excitement was mounting. I might even be able to resume my piano lessons, which I had to stop for lack of money.

The official left. Mother got busy and asked for my help. The piano-room was the first one to suffer a change. It was becoming a bedroom for two, and if the guests had a crib for the baby it would be placed there too, because this was the most spacious room in the house.

Two days later, Mother told me when I came home from school that the official had come again and had given her the exact time of the guests' arrival – they were coming the following afternoon. My sister Raya was furious, as she had to be moved. Of course, so was I. But my curiosity and the excitement of meeting new people were too great for me to worry about future physical discomforts.

It was decided that I should sleep on the small trunk, but that it would be moved to the eating-room. My sister would be sleeping on the floor next to me. The only room that wasn't changed was Mamma's and Papa's bedroom. Since I was the smallest in size, I was promised occasional relief from sleeping in the eating-room by moving to Mamma's bed when Papa was not at home.

The new family arrived. Introductions followed. The Voronovs' first names were Varia and Volodia, nicknames for Varvara and Vladimir. The name of the eight-month-old baby was Annushka. Varia's sister's name was Luba Andreev, short for Lubov, which in Russian means 'love'. She was twenty-two years old and lovely looking, with her large grey eyes and blonde hair. I immediately wanted to be twenty-two. Why did I ever want to be thirteen, such an age of deficiencies? I liked Luba and wanted her to like me.

They brought a lot of food, such as sardines, jams

and cheeses. Living closer to the front made obtaining food easier.

They put most of the goodies on the table and Varia said, 'This is to be eaten by all of us. Please help yourselves to anything that's on the table.'

Mamma thanked her for all of us.

Vladimir Voronov said goodbye shortly after they had arrived. His job as a political adviser required a lot of travelling. He explained it to Mamma as he was saying his farewells. Papa was away when they arrived, so there were all women of different ages and sizes.

Mamma, my sister and I were too bewildered to touch any of the food, but Luba took charge. She put some plates on the table, had all of us sit down and we had an eating feast like we've never had before.

I felt as if we acted freer without the papas dominating the scene. We laughed and ate. We talked as we swallowed and we weren't afraid to be wrong. Maybe it was only I who felt that way.

The following morning I got up early, ready to start a new day. Luba tried to be friendly with my sister and me. Raya didn't show any interest above saying good morning. I was flattered.

After a better than usual breakfast of cocoa and bread with cheese, with plenty of sugar for the cocoa, Luba asked us, 'How would you girls like to show me the town this afternoon when I take Annushka for a walk?'

Raya claimed a previous appointment. I said, 'That should be fun,' even though I hardly knew what I could show her.

When I returned from school Mamma wasn't home. Raya must have gone straight from school to a friend's house. Varia was still unpacking. Luba dressed Annushka, put her in the lovely baby carriage they had brought with them and we were off for our walk.

I began showing Pochep to Luba by telling her that

the neighbourhood of the house we lived in was not considered the best of the city.

'I think it's nice for a small town,' she said. 'You have green trees and not too many horse-drawn carriages, the way they have in some cities in Europe.' This was the first time I had heard Europe mentioned in casual conversation, though I did remember seeing the word 'Europe' in print. It seemed far away, cold and forbidding. When Luba spoke of it, it became alive and inviting.

Not knowing what else to talk about, I continued telling Luba, 'In this town we have neighbourhoods with richer, bigger houses built on hills and smaller ones on the lower streets. I don't know if it would be the same in other towns, since I have only seen two places outside of Pochep.'

'What other places do you know, Hannah? How did you get to know of them?' she asked.

'I visited my aunt who lives in Balaklava, and another aunt in Panurovca.'

I heard Luba laugh. 'Excuse me,' she said, 'but those are funny names.'

I felt that I shouldn't have mentioned these villages to Luba. To erase the bad impression I quickly added, 'My best loved places for walks are the farm on the edge of the river, and a little square in the middle of town where I once watched with great excitement how boys were looking for girls.'

Luba said nothing. And the baby was blissfully asleep. Though I knew that the square wouldn't look the same in the daytime, without the game-playing girls and boys, I promised to take them to the square another time.

The walks grew to be a pleasurable diversion after school. I also felt as if my mind had stretched a little each time, by having to store away a new word, a new name, a new city, thanks to Luba.

On one of our walks I told her how glad I was to

have them all staying with us, and how kind I thought
they were, to which Luba answered, 'Civilised people
should share material goods whenever they can with
those who have less. We knew that in your part of
the world people didn't have enough to eat because
everything had to be sent to the front.'

Since I had not heard the word 'civilised' used that
way before, I asked Luba, 'What does that word actually
mean?'

'To me,' said Luba, 'it means to be aware of human
conditions around you and to do what you can to
improve them.'

That made me think. I tried to improve my mother's
conditions by cleaning and scrubbing. If 'human' means
everybody, how could I help? But I wanted to know
more about it.

When we got back from our walk Luba took out the
atlas, called me, and, turning the pages, found a map of
Russia. She showed me a little dot where the name
'Pochep' could be seen, and said, 'This is where we are
now. Look how small that dot is, Hannah, compared
with the maps of all the countries on this earth.'

My face must have shown amazement and disbelief.
Finally, I said in a low voice, 'Here we are tucked away
in a place that doesn't take more than a dot on the map,
and we probably are destined not to see more . . .' I felt
like crying.

Luba hugged me, and her reassurances were like a ray
of sunshine on a stormy day. She turned her smiling
face toward me and said, 'You, Hannah, you *will* see
more. You have enough curiosity to send you to the
moon.'

I took her hand and shook it vigorously. 'Thank you,
Luba, you make me feel good,' I whispered, not wanting
anyone else to hear me.

When we returned to the eating-room, the samovar
was steaming cosily and everyone was sitting around

the table ready for the evening's light meal and tea. Varia must have invited Mamma to join them. Usually the Voronovs had their meal first because of Annushka.

Mamma had said, 'When there is a baby, she should come first.'

No one had argued the case. On school days, six days a week, Raya and I were at school until three in the afternoon.

The hardest times were when the men were at home. The women tried to stay out of their way, each one in her own corner. Once we overheard their discussion about the war.

'Volodia,' asked Papa, 'why are you against your own country? You want Germany to win? Why?'

'Germany is a country of culture. They are good to the Jewish people. They didn't start the war; let them win it.'

Volodia was getting angry. 'It's no use arguing with you,' he yelled. 'You don't use reason.' They stayed angry with each other until they had to leave.

Luba and I didn't like what we heard. Volodia and Papa didn't get along, but why? I couldn't understand. I didn't dare to ask Luba, but I saw that she too was disturbed by it.

Of the women, Mamma enjoyed our guests least of all. No matter what subject the women talked about, for example if it were clothes, Mother had nothing of interest to display. Luba and Varia had a few outfits one could be envious of, and I enjoyed seeing them when we were playing fashion games.

I felt that Mamma wasn't pleased to see my growing friendship with Luba. I wondered why. Could it be because she wasn't Jewish? The question of religion never came up between the two families. Varia and the rest of them were not church-going people, but Mamma did feel a little uncomfortable about kosher foods and the preparation of the Sabbath dinners, which were cooked on Friday.

My sister Raya was in a continuous stew about one thing or another in connection with the Voronovs. If it wasn't about their fashionable clothes then it would be about the tempting smells that came from the kitchen as they were preparing their meals. When she had nothing else to complain about she would begin milking me by asking, 'What does Luba talk to you about on your walks? How can she be friends with you? You are still a baby. She is almost old enough to be your mother.' At which point she would start laughing, and I would run away from her in tears.

For me, each day brought something new to think about. I did miss my piano playing. Annushka's crib, being in the piano-room, made my piano playing almost impossible, for she had to take several naps a day. Because I was bashful about my playing I could only play when our guests were out. A few times I played Bach for Luba, who urged me to play more. Still, my reluctance to play for people persisted.

During the Easter vacation, school was closed for just a few days. The dates of Easter and Passover didn't coincide that year. The house was crowded. Both men, Papa and Volodia, were home. The job of taking Annushka for a walk was gladly taken over by Volodia.

Luba offered to take me to a new place that had just opened. It was called *Cinematograph*. There, several times a day, one could see still photographs of faraway places, with the man who was showing them explaining each one. Pathé-Journal got the credits for the photographs on the screen. The entrance price was twenty-five Kopeks.

Luba had been to some of the places we saw. When we came out she was as excited as I was, talking fast, she said to me, 'I didn't want to speak while the man was explaining the pictures, but I want you to know more about these cities.' She explained that they had music played by big symphony orchestras, and paintings and sculptures collected in large museums, and she described the beauty of their oceans and mountains.

I interrupted her. 'The last two names are the only ones I know from studying geography, a subject I didn't care for too much.'

It was a very exciting afternoon. I didn't mind being thirteen. When we got back I remembered my other friend – my Diary. I found a little empty corner in the crowded house and went on saying things I couldn't say to Luba.

Dear Diary,
It has been long, I know, but here I am. My new friend, Luba, at twenty-two, doesn't mind being friends with me. She is very nice with large grey eyes, long eyelashes, blonde hair, and, you'll never guess, she has a short, man's haircut – very becoming. When I asked her why so short, her answer was, 'Lice don't live in short hair; they feel too exposed to the elements.'

She knows so much about so many things and likes to talk about them. I want to be part of the bigger world that I don't know, not only of the little dot on the Russian map. Luba thinks I will. She said the war will be over soon, now that America was planning to join it and Germany was losing battle after battle.

Oh, DD, to have time to learn, to see, to hear, to love – things, people. I might even be able to go back to Madame Smirnova since the nice family has been given money by the government to pay us for their lodgings and we, in turn, will have more money to live on. I am changing, DD. Now that I have a goal, to see more of the world I live in, I don't even mind my sister not wanting to take me along with her. She might have dreams of her own. I do want to hear my mother laugh more. But the important thing is to live, to grow, to learn Bach's music and maths and logic, Luba will help me to get there . . . and everywhere!

Notes

1 The revolution of 1905, which was crushed.

2 *Mezuzah*: a small piece of metal containing a scroll of parchment with the words: 'Listen Israel, God is One' written on it.

3 The name of the city was Pahar, from the Russian word for fire, *pojar*.

4 *Kalitka*: a small door leading to a yard, in the middle of which stands a house.

5 *Paravay*: from the Hebrew *parev*, or 'neutral', meaning foods such as fruit, vegetables, fish and eggs, which can all be eaten with meat or milk.